Regionalism, Multilateralism, and Deeper Integration

Integrating National Economies: Promise and Pitfalls

Robert Z. Lawrence (Harvard University), Albert Bressand (Promethee), and Takatoshi Ito (Hitotsubashi University)
A VISION FOR THE WORLD ECONOMY: OPENNESS, DIVERSITY, AND COHESION

Robert Z. Lawrence

Regionalism, Multilateralism, and Deeper Integration

THE BROOKINGS INSTITUTION
Washington, D.C.

Library of Congress Cataloging-in-Publication data:
Lawrence, Robert Z., 1949–
Regionalism, multilateralism, and deeper integration /
Robert Z. Lawrence.
p. cm. — (Integrating national economies)
Includes bibliographical references and index.
ISBN 0-8157-5182-6 (cl: alk. paper). ISBN 0-8157-5181-8 (pa: alk. paper)
1. International economic integration—Case studies. 2. Regionalism—
Case studies. 3. Free trade—Case studies. I. Brookings Institution.
II. Title. III. Series.
HF 1418.5.L388 1995
337—dc20   95-26205
                                                                  CIP

9 8 7 6 5 4 3 2 1

The paper used in this publication meets the minimum requirements of
American National Standard for Information Sciences—Permanence of Paper
for Printed Library Materials, ANSI Z39.48-1984

Typeset in Plantin

Composition by Princeton Editorial Associates
Princeton, New Jersey

Printed by R. R. Donnelley and Sons Co.
Harrisonburg, Virginia

The Brookings Institution is an independent organization devoted to nonpartisan research, education, and publication in economics, government, foreign policy, and the social sciences generally. Its principal purposes are to aid in the development of sound public policies and to promote public understanding of issues of national importance.

The Institution was founded on December 8, 1927, to merge the activities of the Institute for Government Research, founded in 1916, the Institute of Economics, founded in 1922, and the Robert Brookings Graduate School of Economics and Government, founded in 1924.

The Board of Trustees is responsible for the general administration of the Institution, while the immediate direction of the policies, program, and staff is vested in the President, assisted by an advisory committee of the officers and staff. The by-laws of the Institution state: "It is the function of the Trustees to make possible the conduct of scientific research, and publication, under the most favorable conditions, and to safeguard the independence of the research staff in the pursuit of their studies and in the publication of the results of such studies. It is not a part of their function to determine, control, or influence the conduct of particular investigations or the conclusions reached."

The President bears final responsibility for the decision to publish a manuscript as a Brookings book. In reaching his judgment on the competence, accuracy, and objectivity of each study, the President is advised by the director of the appropriate research program and weighs the views of a panel of expert outside readers who report to him in confidence on the quality of the work. Publication of a work signifies that it is deemed a competent treatment worthy of public consideration but does not imply endorsement of conclusions or recommendations.

The Institution maintains its position of neutrality on issues of public policy in order to safeguard the intellectual freedom of the staff. Hence interpretations or conclusions in Brookings publications should be understood to be solely those of the authors and should not be attributed to the Institution, to its trustees, officers, or other staff members, or to the organizations that support its research.

Foreword

D URING THE PAST decade policymakers have pursued international economic liberalization through both multilateral and regional arrangements. In the World Trade Organization, more than one hundred governments have pledged greater open trade in goods and services. The European Union and the North American Free Trade Agreement are prominent examples of preferential, or regional, arrangements.

Arguments rage as to whether regional arrangements undercut or contribute to a more successful international economy. In this book, Robert Z. Lawrence argues that neither past experience nor traditional trade theory provides an adequate guide to answering these questions. In the 1930s, for instance, countries sought to withdraw from the world economy, and in the 1950s and 1960s some developing countries promoted import substitution rather than export and foreign investment policies. Today regional arrangements generally seek to facilitate their members' participation in the world economy. The traditional theoretical view of preferential trading arrangements focuses on their impact on border barriers. But this overlooks many features of deeper international integration that these recent arrangements cover.

Lawrence analyzes and compares the achievements and major risks of regional arrangements in Europe, America, and the Asia Pacific. Evolving regional arrangements could result in new forms of protectionism through rules of origin and antidumping and countervailing duties. However, some regional arrangements are open to enlargement, and good ones create incentives for expansion. Regionalism is here to stay, says the author, so keeping arrangements open must be a primary objective.

Lawrence is grateful to Henry Aaron for extensive comments on the first draft of this study. He also especially thanks Louka Katseli, Yung Chul Park, and other participants in a conference held at Brookings in fall 1993, and Pillar Maisterrsa for research assistance.

At Brookings Theresa Walker edited the manuscript, Gerard Trimarco verified it, and Mark M. Steese and Evelyn M. E. Taylor provided administrative assistance. Princeton Editorial Associates prepared the index.

Funding for the project came from the Center for Global Partnership of the Japan Foundation, the Curry Foundation, the Ford Foundation, the Korea Foundation, the Tokyo Club Foundation for Global Studies, the United States-Japan Foundation, and the Alex C. Walker Educational and Charitable Foundation. The author and Brookings are grateful for their support.

The views expressed in this book are those of the author and should not be attributed to any of the persons or organizations acknowledged above, or to the trustees, officers, or other staff members of the Brookings Institution.

MICHAEL H. ARMACOST
President

February 1996
Washington, D.C.

Contents

Preface to the Studies on Integrating National Economies

*E*CONOMIC interdependence among nations has increased sharply in the past half century. For example, while the value of total production of industrial countries increased at a rate of about 9 percent a year on average between 1964 and 1992, the value of the exports of those nations grew at an average rate of 12 percent, and lending and borrowing across national borders through banks surged upward even more rapidly at 23 percent a year. This international economic interdependence has contributed to significantly improved standards of living for most countries. Continuing international economic integration holds out the promise of further benefits. Yet the increasing sensitivity of national economies to events and policies originating abroad creates dilemmas and pitfalls if national policies and international cooperation are poorly managed.

The Brookings Project on Integrating National Economies, of which this study is a component, focuses on the interplay between two fundamental facts about the world at the end of the twentieth century. First, the world will continue for the foreseeable future to be organized politically into nation-states with sovereign governments. Second, increasing economic integration among nations will continue to erode differences among national economies and undermine the autonomy of national governments. The project explores the opportunities and tensions arising from these two facts.

Scholars from a variety of disciplines have produced twenty-one studies for the first phase of the project. Each study examines the heightened competition between national political sovereignty and increased cross-border economic integration. This preface identifies background themes and issues common to all the studies and provides a brief overview of the project as a whole.[1]

Increasing World Economic Integration

Two underlying sets of causes have led nations to become more closely intertwined. First, technological, social, and cultural changes have sharply reduced the effective economic distances among nations. Second, many of the government policies that traditionally inhibited cross-border transactions have been relaxed or even dismantled.

The same improvements in transportation and communications technology that make it much easier and cheaper for companies in New York to ship goods to California, for residents of Strasbourg to visit relatives in Marseilles, and for investors in Hokkaido to buy and sell shares on the Tokyo Stock Exchange facilitate trade, migration, and capital movements spanning nations and continents. The sharply reduced costs of moving goods, money, people, and information underlie the profound economic truth that technology has made the world markedly smaller.

New communications technology has been especially significant for financial activity. Computers, switching devices, and telecommunications satellites have slashed the cost of transmitting information internationally, of confirming transactions, and of paying for transactions. In the 1950s, for example, foreign exchange could be bought and sold only during conventional business hours in the initiating party's time zone. Such transactions can now be carried out instantaneously twenty-four hours a day. Large banks pass the management of their worldwide foreign-exchange positions around the globe from one branch to another, staying continuously ahead of the setting sun.

Such technological innovations have increased the knowledge of potentially profitable international exchanges and of economic op-

---

1. A complete list of authors and study titles is included at the beginning of this volume, facing the title page.

portunities abroad. Those developments, in turn, have changed consumers' and producers' tastes. Foreign goods, foreign vacations, foreign financial investments—virtually anything from other nations—have lost some of their exotic character.

Although technological change permits increased contact among nations, it would not have produced such dramatic effects if it had been countermanded by government policies. Governments have traditionally taxed goods moving in international trade, directly restricted imports and subsidized exports, and tried to limit international capital movements. Those policies erected "separation fences" at the borders of nations. From the perspective of private sector agents, separation fences imposed extra costs on cross-border transactions. They reduced trade and, in some cases, eliminated it. During the 1930s governments used such policies with particular zeal, a practice now believed to have deepened and lengthened the Great Depression.

After World War II, most national governments began—sometimes unilaterally, more often collaboratively—to lower their separation fences, to make them more permeable, or sometimes even to tear down parts of them. The multilateral negotiations under the auspices of the General Agreement on Trade and Tariffs (GATT)—for example, the Kennedy Round in the 1960s, the Tokyo Round in the 1970s, and most recently the protracted negotiations of the Uruguay Round, formally signed only in April 1994—stand out as the most prominent examples of fence lowering for trade in goods. Though contentious and marked by many compromises, the GATT negotiations are responsible for sharp reductions in at-the-border restrictions on trade in goods and services. After the mid-1980s a large number of developing countries moved unilaterally to reduce border barriers and to pursue outwardly oriented policies.

The lowering of fences for financial transactions began later and was less dramatic. Nonetheless, by the 1990s government restrictions on capital flows, especially among the industrial countries, were much less important and widespread than at the end of World War II and in the 1950s.

By shrinking the economic distances among nations, changes in technology would have progressively integrated the world economy even in the absence of reductions in governments' separation fences. Reductions in separation fences would have enhanced interdependence even without the technological innovations. Together, these two sets of evolutionary changes have reinforced each other and strikingly transformed the world economy.

Changes in the Government of Nations

Simultaneously with the transformation of the global economy, major changes have occurred in the world's political structure. First, the number of governmental decisionmaking units in the world has expanded markedly, and political power has been diffused more broadly among them. Rising nationalism and, in some areas, heightened ethnic tensions have accompanied that increasing political pluralism.

The history of membership in international organizations documents the sharp growth in the number of independent states. For example, only 44 nations participated in the Bretton Woods conference of July 1944, which gave birth to the International Monetary Fund. But by the end of 1970, the IMF had 118 member nations. The number of members grew to 150 by the mid-1980s and to 178 by December 1993. Much of this growth reflects the collapse of colonial empires. Although many nations today are small and carry little individual weight in the global economy, their combined influence is considerable, and their interests cannot be ignored as easily as they were in the past.

A second political trend, less visible but equally important, has been the gradual loss of the political and economic hegemony of the United States. Immediately after World War II, the United States by itself accounted for more than one-third of world production. By the early 1990s the U.S. share had fallen to about one-fifth. Concurrently, the political and economic influence of the European colonial powers continued to wane, and the economic significance of nations outside Europe and North America, such as Japan, Korea, Indonesia, China, Brazil, and Mexico, increased. A world in which economic power and influence are widely diffused has displaced a world in which one or a few nations effectively dominated international decisionmaking.

Turmoil and the prospect of fundamental change in the formerly centrally planned economies compose a third factor causing radical changes in world politics. During the era of central planning, governments in those nations tried to limit external influences on their economies. Now leaders in the formerly planned economies are trying to adopt reforms modeled on Western capitalist principles. To the extent that these efforts succeed, those nations will increase their economic involvement with the rest of the world. Political and economic alignments among the Western industrialized nations will be forced to adapt.

Governments and scholars have begun to assess these three trends, but their far-reaching ramifications will not be clear for decades.

Dilemmas for National Policies

Cross-border economic integration and national political sovereignty have increasingly come into conflict, leading to a growing mismatch between the economic and political structures of the world. The effective domains of economic markets have come to coincide less and less with national governmental jurisdictions.

When the separation fences at nations' borders were high, governments and citizens could sharply distinguish "international" from "domestic" policies. International policies dealt with at-the-border barriers, such as tariffs and quotas, or responded to events occurring abroad. In contrast, domestic policies were concerned with everything behind the nation's borders, such as competition and antitrust rules, corporate governance, product standards, worker safety, regulation and supervision of financial institutions, environmental protection, tax codes, and the government's budget. Domestic policies were regarded as matters about which nations were sovereign, to be determined by the preferences of the nation's citizens and its political institutions, without regard for effects on other nations.

As separation fences have been lowered and technological innovations have shrunk economic distances, a multitude of formerly neglected differences among nations' domestic policies have become exposed to international scrutiny. National governments and international negotiations must thus increasingly deal with "deeper"—behind-the-border—integration. For example, if country A permits companies to emit air and water pollutants whereas country B does not, companies that use pollution-generating methods of production will find it cheaper to produce in country A. Companies in country B that compete internationally with companies in country A are likely to complain that foreign competitors enjoy unfair advantages and to press for international pollution standards.

Deeper integration requires analysis of the economic and the political aspects of virtually all nonborder policies and practices. Such issues have already figured prominently in negotiations over the evolution of the European Community, over the Uruguay Round of GATT negotiations, over the North American Free Trade Agreement (NAFTA), and over the bilateral economic relationships between Japan and the United States. Future debates about behind-the-border policies will occur with increasing frequency and prove at least as complex and contentious as the past negotiations regarding at-the-border restrictions.

Tensions about deeper integration arise from three broad sources: cross-border spillovers, diminished national autonomy, and challenges to political sovereignty.

Cross-Border Spillovers

Some activities in one nation produce consequences that spill across borders and affect other nations. Illustrations of these spillovers abound. Given the impact of modern technology of banking and securities markets in creating interconnected networks, lax rules in one nation erode the ability of all other nations to enforce banking and securities rules and to deal with fraudulent transactions. Given the rapid diffusion of knowledge, science and technology policies in one nation generate knowledge that other nations can use without full payment. Labor market policies become matters of concern to other nations because workers migrate in search of work; policies in one nation can trigger migration that floods or starves labor markets elsewhere. When one nation dumps pollutants into the air or water that other nations breathe or drink, the matter goes beyond the unitary concern of the polluting nation and becomes a matter for international negotiation. Indeed, the hydrocarbons that are emitted into the atmosphere when individual nations burn coal for generating electricity contribute to global warming and are thereby a matter of concern for the entire world.

The tensions associated with cross-border spillovers can be especially vexing when national policies generate outcomes alleged to be competitively inequitable, as in the example in which country A permits companies to emit pollutants and country B does not. Or consider a situation in which country C requires commodities, whether produced at home or abroad, to meet certain design standards, justified for safety reasons. Foreign competitors may find it too expensive to meet these standards. In that event, the standards in C act very much like tariffs or quotas, effectively narrowing or even eliminating foreign competition for domestic producers. Citing examples of this sort, producers or governments in individual nations often complain that business is not conducted on a "level playing field." Typically, the complaining nation proposes that *other* nations adjust their policies to moderate or remove the competitive inequities.

Arguments for creating a level playing field are troublesome at best. International trade occurs precisely because of differences among nations—in resource endowments, labor skills, and consumer tastes. Nations specialize in producing goods and services in which they are relatively most efficient. In a fundamental sense, cross-border trade is valuable because the playing field is *not* level.

When David Ricardo first developed the theory of comparative advantage, he focused on differences among nations owing to climate or technology. But Ricardo could as easily have ascribed the productive differences to differing "social climates" as to physical or technological climates. Taking all "climatic" differences as given, the theory of comparative advantage argues that free trade among nations will maximize global welfare.

Taken to its logical extreme, the notion of leveling the playing field implies that nations should become homogeneous in all major respects. But that recommendation is unrealistic and even pernicious. Suppose country A decides that it is too poor to afford the costs of a clean environment, and will thus permit the production of goods that pollute local air and water supplies. Or suppose it concludes that it cannot afford stringent protections for worker safety. Country A will then argue that it is inappropriate for other nations to impute to country A the value they themselves place on a clean environment and safety standards (just as it would be inappropriate to impute the A valuations to the environment of other nations). The core of the idea of political sovereignty is to permit national residents to order their lives and property in accord with their own preferences.

Which perspective about differences among nations in behind-the-border policies is more compelling? Is country A merely exercising its national preferences and appropriately exploiting its comparative advantage in goods that are dirty or dangerous to produce? Or does a legitimate international problem exist that justifies pressure from other nations urging country A to accept changes in its policies (thus curbing its national sovereignty)? When national governments negotiate resolutions to such questions—trying to agree whether individual nations are legitimately exercising sovereign choices or, alternatively, engaging in behavior that is unfair or damaging to other nations—the dialogue is invariably contentious because the resolutions depend on the typically complex circumstances of the international spillovers and on the relative weights accorded to the interests of particular individuals and particular nations.

Diminished National Autonomy

As cross-border economic integration increases, governments experience greater difficulties in trying to control events within their borders. Those difficulties, summarized by the term *diminished autonomy*, are the second set of reasons why tensions arise from the competition between political sovereignty and economic integration.

For example, nations adjust monetary and fiscal policies to influence domestic inflation and employment. In setting these policies, smaller countries have always been somewhat constrained by foreign economic events and policies. Today, however, all nations are constrained, often severely. More than in the past, therefore, nations may be better able to achieve their economic goals if they work together collaboratively in adjusting their macroeconomic policies.

Diminished autonomy and cross-border spillovers can sometimes be allowed to persist without explicit international cooperation to deal with them. States in the United States adopt their own tax systems and set policies for assistance to poor single people without any formal cooperation or limitation. Market pressures operate to force a degree of de facto cooperation. If one state taxes corporations too heavily, it knows business will move elsewhere. (Those familiar with older debates about "fiscal federalism" within the United States and other nations will recognize the similarity between those issues and the emerging international debates about deeper integration of national economies.) Analogously, differences among nations in regulations, standards, policies, institutions, and even social and cultural preferences create economic incentives for a kind of arbitrage that erodes or eliminates the differences. Such pressures involve not only the conventional arbitrage that exploits price differentials (buying at one point in geographic space or time and selling at another) but also shifts in the location of production facilities and in the residence of factors of production.

In many other cases, however, cross-border spillovers, arbitrage pressures, and diminished effectiveness of national policies can produce unwanted consequences. In cases involving what economists call externalities (external economies and diseconomies), national governments may need to cooperate to promote mutual interests. For example, population growth, continued urbanization, and the more intensive exploitation of natural resources generate external diseconomies not only within but across national boundaries. External economies generated when benefits spill across national jurisdictions probably also increase in importance (for instance, the gains from basic research and from control of communicable diseases).

None of these situations is new, but technological change and the reduction of tariffs and quotas heighten their importance. When one nation produces goods (such as scientific research) or "bads" (such as pollution) that significantly affect other nations, individual governments acting sequentially and noncooperatively cannot deal effectively with the resulting issues. In the absence of explicit cooperation and political leadership, too few collective goods and too many collective bads will be supplied.

Challenges to Political Sovereignty

The pressures from cross-border economic integration sometimes even lead individuals or governments to challenge the core assumptions of national political sovereignty. Such challenges are a third source of tensions about deeper integration.

The existing world system of nation-states assumes that a nation's residents are free to follow their own values and to select their own political arrangements without interference from others. Similarly, property rights are allocated by nation. (The so-called global commons, such as outer space and the deep seabed, are the sole exceptions.) A nation is assumed to have the sovereign right to exploit its property in accordance with its own preferences and policies. Political sovereignty is thus analogous to the concept of consumer sovereignty (the presumption that the individual consumer best knows his or her own interests and should exercise them freely).

In times of war, some nations have had sovereignty wrested from them by force. In earlier eras, a handful of individuals or groups have questioned the premises of political sovereignty. With the profound increases in economic integration in recent decades, however, a larger number of individuals and groups—and occasionally even their national governments—have identified circumstances in which, it is claimed, some universal or international set of values should take precedence over the preferences or policies of particular nations.

Some groups seize on human-rights issues, for example, or what they deem to be egregiously inappropriate political arrangements in other nations. An especially prominent case occurred when citizens in many nations labeled the former apartheid policies of South Africa an affront to universal values and emphasized

that the South African government was not legitimately representing the interests of a majority of South Africa's residents. Such
views caused many national governments to apply economic sanctions against South Africa. Examples of value conflicts are not
restricted to human rights, however. Groups focusing on environmental issues characterize tropical rain forests as the lungs of the
world and the genetic repository for numerous species of plants
and animals that are the heritage of all mankind. Such views lead
Europeans, North Americans, or Japanese to challenge the timber-
cutting policies of Brazilians and Indonesians. A recent controversy over tuna fishing with long drift nets that kill porpoises is yet
another example. Environmentalists in the United States whose
sensibilities were offended by the drowning of porpoises required
U.S. boats at some additional expense to amend their fishing
practices. The U.S. fishermen, complaining about imported tuna
caught with less regard for porpoises, persuaded the U.S. government to ban such tuna imports (both direct imports from the
countries in which the tuna is caught and indirect imports shipped
via third countries). Mexico and Venezuela were the main countries affected by this ban; a GATT dispute panel sided with Mexico against the United States in the controversy, which further
upset the U.S. environmental community.

A common feature of all such examples is the existence, real or
alleged, of "psychological externalities" or "political failures." Those
holding such views reject untrammeled political sovereignty for nation-states in deference to universal or non-national values. They
wish to constrain the exercise of individual nations' sovereignties
through international negotiations or, if necessary, by even stronger
intervention.

The Management of International Convergence

In areas in which arbitrage pressures and cross-border spillovers
are weak and psychological or political externalities are largely
absent, national governments may encounter few problems with
deeper integration. Diversity across nations may persist quite easily. But at the other extreme, arbitrage and spillovers in some areas

may be so strong that they threaten to erode national diversity completely. Or psychological and political sensitivities may be asserted too powerfully to be ignored. Governments will then be confronted with serious tensions, and national policies and behaviors may eventually converge to common, worldwide patterns (for example, subject to internationally agreed norms or minimum standards). Eventual convergence across nations, if it occurs, could happen in a harmful way (national policies and practices being driven to a least common denominator with externalities ignored, in effect a "race to the bottom") or it could occur with mutually beneficial results ("survival of the fittest and the best").

Each study in this series addresses basic questions about the management of international convergence: if, when, and how national governments should intervene to try to influence the consequences of arbitrage pressures, cross-border spillovers, diminished autonomy, and the assertion of psychological or political externalities. A wide variety of responses is conceivable. We identify six, which should be regarded not as distinct categories but as ranges along a continuum.

National autonomy defines a situation at one end of the continuum in which national governments make decentralized decisions with little or no consultation and no explicit cooperation. This response represents political sovereignty at its strongest, undiluted by any international management of convergence.

Mutual recognition, like national autonomy, presumes decentralized decisions by national governments and relies on market competition to guide the process of international convergence. Mutual recognition, however, entails exchanges of information and consultations among governments to constrain the formation of national regulations and policies. As understood in discussions of economic integration within the European Community, moreover, mutual recognition entails an explicit acceptance by each member nation of the regulations, standards, and certification procedures of other members. For example, mutual recognition allows wine or liquor produced in any European Union country to be sold in all twelve member countries even if production standards in member countries differ. Doctors licensed in France are permitted to practice in

Germany, and vice versa, even if licensing procedures in the two countries differ.

Governments may agree on rules that restrict their freedom to set policy or that promote gradual convergence in the structure of policy. As international consultations and monitoring of compliance with such rules become more important, this situation can be described as *monitored decentralization*. The Group of Seven finance ministers meetings, supplemented by the IMF's surveillance over exchange rate and macroeconomic policies, illustrate this approach to management.

Coordination goes further than mutual recognition and monitored decentralization in acknowledging convergence pressures. It is also more ambitious in promoting intergovernmental cooperation to deal with them. Coordination involves jointly designed mutual adjustments of national policies. In clear-cut cases of coordination, bargaining occurs and governments agree to behave differently from the ways they would have behaved without the agreement. Examples include the World Health Organization's procedures for controlling communicable diseases and the 1987 Montreal Protocol (to a 1985 framework convention) for the protection of stratospheric ozone by reducing emissions of chlorofluorocarbons.

Explicit harmonization, which requires still higher levels of intergovernmental cooperation, may require agreement on regional standards or world standards. Explicit harmonization typically entails still greater departures from decentralization in decision-making and still further strengthening of international institutions. The 1988 agreement among major central banks to set minimum standards for the required capital positions of commercial banks (reached through the Committee on Banking Regulations and Supervisory Practices at the Bank for International Settlements) is an example of partially harmonized regulations.

At the opposite end of the spectrum from national autonomy lies *federalist mutual governance*, which implies continuous bargaining and joint, centralized decisionmaking. To make federalist mutual governance work would require greatly strengthened supranational institutions. This end of the management spectrum, now relevant only as an analytical benchmark, is a possible outcome that can be imagined for the middle or late decades of the twenty-first century, possibly even sooner for regional groupings like the European Union.

Overview of the Brookings Project

Despite their growing importance, the issues of deeper economic integration and its competition with national political sovereignty were largely neglected in the 1980s. In 1992 the Brookings Institution initiated its project on Integrating National Economies to direct attention to these important questions.

In studying this topic, Brookings sought and received the cooperation of some of the world's leading economists, political scientists, foreign-policy specialists, and government officials, representing all regions of the world. Although some functional areas require a special focus on European, Japanese, and North American perspectives, at all junctures the goal was to include, in addition, the perspectives of developing nations and the formerly centrally planned economies.

The first phase of the project commissioned the twenty-one scholarly studies listed at the beginning of the book. One or two lead discussants, typically residents of parts of the world other than the area where the author resides, were asked to comment on each study.

Authors enjoyed substantial freedom to design their individual studies, taking due account of the overall themes and goals of the project. The guidelines for the studies requested that at least some of the analysis be carried out with a non-normative perspective. In effect, authors were asked to develop a "baseline" of what might happen in the absence of changed policies or further international cooperation. For their normative analyses, authors were asked to start with an agnostic posture that did not prejudge the net benefits or costs resulting from integration. The project organizers themselves had no presumption about whether national diversity is better or worse than international convergence or about what the individual studies should conclude regarding the desirability of increased integration. On the contrary, each author was asked to address the trade-offs in his or her issue area between diversity and convergence and to locate the area, currently and prospectively, on the spectrum of international management possibilities running between national autonomy through mutual recognition to co-ordination and explicit harmonization.

HENRY J. AARON   SUSAN M. COLLINS
RALPH C. BRYANT   ROBERT Z. LAWRENCE

Regionalism, Multilateralism, and Deeper Integration

Chapter 1

Introduction

O VER THE PAST DECADE, international economic liberalization has been pursued through both multilateral and regional agreements. In the Uruguay Round, negotiated between 1986 and 1993, more than one hundred governments agreed to new rules for more open trade in goods and services. They also established a new World Trade Organization (WTO) with enhanced enforcement power. At the same time, however, many regional economic arrangements have been negotiated. The most well-known ones are the program of the European Union to complete its internal market program (EC 92) and the United States, Canada, and Mexico to form the North American Free Trade Agreement (NAFTA), but these were only the most prominent of a rapidly growing number of preferential economic agreements that have emerged or been revitalized in recent years. The International Monetary Fund compiled a list of such agreements numbering sixty-eight in 1994.[1] It covers all five continents, running virtually the full alphabet from the ASEAN Free Trade Area (AFTA) and the Andean Pact (ANCOM) to the Central African Customs Union (UDEAC) and the West African Economic and Monetary Union (WAEMU). It is estimated that about 90 percent of all the contracting parties in the General Agreement on Tariffs and Trade (GATT) are signatories to such arrangements.[2]

1. IMF (1994, pp. 107–116).
2. Japan, Hong Kong, and India are among a mere ten or so exceptions. See Japan (1995, p. 304).

1

Regional Arrangements: Building Blocks or Stumbling Blocks?

These trends combine to raise the central question of this book: are globalization and regionalization complementary or conflicting developments? In other words, are these regional arrangements stumbling blocks or building blocks for a more integrated and successful international economy?[3]

The answer is hotly debated. Some pessimists see the current situation as an ominous precursor of what has come before. They believe that the world trading system is fragmenting in the same way as it did in the 1930s.[4] The rule-based multilateral trading system that has developed under the GATT will be destroyed as Europe, North America, and Asia become "fortresses" in which some trading partners obtain refuge, while others are excluded. In his bestselling book, *Head to Head,* Lester Thurow, for example, proclaimed that "GATT is dead" and argued that the world would shift to a tripolar system with three blocs centered on Europe, the United States, and Japan, which would have free trade internally but managed trade among them.[5]

Multilateralists, such as Jagdish Bhagwati, are not willing to give GATT the last rites but remain concerned that the expansion of regionalism will undermine the multilateral system and weaken its thrust toward liberalization.[6] Bhagwati fears that if some countries are given a vested interest in preferential arrangements, they will have less incentive to press for complete free trade. If leaders devote resources and political capital to their regional arrangements, they could be diverted from investing in the multilateral system. He concedes that regional arrangements may have played a role in spurring the completion of the Uruguay Round. But he argues that now that the round has been successfully completed, the WTO should be the sole locus of future trade liberalization.

3. I owe this expression to Jagdish Bhagwati.

4. For estimates of the impact of a fortress European Community or United States see Stoeckel, Pearce, and Banks (1990).

5. Thurow (1992, p. 65).

6. See Bhagwati (1992, 1994b); Bhagwati and Krueger (1995).

Bhagwati therefore calls for greater disciplines on preferential arrangements and a more exclusive reliance on global initiatives.

Some views of the process are more sanguine. Regional arrangements have also been presented as a complement and supplement to liberalization under the multilateral trading system. Indeed, this is the traditional view enshrined in Article 24 of GATT, which permits the formation of preferential trading arrangements such as free trade areas and customs unions provided they meet certain conditions. It is also the view of most American trade officials. By following *both* regional and multilateral approaches, they argue, world trade liberalization can proceed more rapidly.[7] Such a multispeed approach to freer trade can achieve greater gains for those willing to proceed faster and at the same time put pressure on the multilateral track to perform better.

Even if they do not erect new barriers, or thwart multilateral liberalization, the emergence of these arrangements could lead to some undesirable outcomes. Major regional arrangements could be dominated by considerations of market power rather than the principles of a liberal trading order. In a scenario called "imperial harmonization," the world economy is dominated by two major regional arrangements, one led by the United States, the other by the European Union (EU).[8] Other nations either sign up and play by the rules of one or the other, or they remain left out in the cold. Although such an outcome allows for closer economic ties among participants, the rules of the game are determined in the United States and the EU and do not reflect the needs or wishes of others. Each dominant economy becomes the center or hub in which other members are simply spokes. The system has insiders and outsiders. This world mirrors the fears of Louka T. Katseli, who argues that regional arrangements will lead to thick networks of nations and firms linked by trade and investment, providing bene-

---

7. According to Mickey Kantor, the United States special trade representative, "Regional trading arrangements . . . can prepare developing nations for admittance to the global trading system . . . [and] . . . they can . . . complement global trading . . . and lubricate negotiations." "Global Village Gathers Speed," *Financial Times,* October 13, 1993, p. 31.

8. Lawrence, Bressand, and Ito (1996).

fits to those who are part of these networks but increasingly marginalizing those who are left out.[9]

Theory and Experience

Indeed, both theory and experience provide reasons why this controversy is not easily resolved. Economic theory suggests that the optimal free trade area is the world. Multilateral free trade allows for the operation of a single set of nondiscriminatory rules to govern all trade. However, achieving such liberalization multilaterally in large negotiations that extend benefits unconditionally to all participating nations may prove difficult. Since they are very important, large countries that are reluctant to liberalize—footdraggers—can stall the entire process. Since they are relatively insignificant, small countries—free riders—have incentives to take the benefits without making concessions of their own. Moreover, obtaining an international consensus on the rules of the game may prove impossible.

The theoretical judgment of regional trade arrangements is also ambivalent.[10] As Jacob Viner pointed out, preferential free trade arrangements can have beneficial and detrimental effects on welfare.[11] They move the world both closer to and further away from complete free trade. On the one hand, by eliminating the barriers among its members, an arrangement can *create* trade and improve efficiency by shifting production from a high-cost domestic producer to a lower-cost trading partner. On the other hand, by granting members market access on preferential terms, it can *divert* trade, by expanding the production of less efficient members and reducing the production of more efficient outsiders. Economic theory also provides no firm guidance on whether these arrangements are likely to prevent or accelerate further multi-

9. Katseli (1992).

10. Indeed it was theorizing about regional arrangements that led Lipsey and Lancaster (1956) to derive their general theory of the second best, which states that when there are two or more obstacles to achieving an efficient outcome, the removal of only one or some of them does not necessarily improve welfare.

11. Viner (1950).

lateral liberalization. Various models suggest that forces are operating in both directions.[12]

The postwar experience with both multilateralism and regionalism has been mixed. On the one hand, the multilateral trading system has enjoyed spectacular success in lowering trade barriers on industrial products. The General Agreement on Tariffs and Trade enshrined the principles of nondiscrimination among its contracting parties. In a series of trade rounds, GATT members reduced their tariffs and developed codes of conduct to govern trade. The most ambitious of these, the Uruguay Round, ended in 1993. Besides further lowering tariffs, its members agreed to begin liberalizing agricultural trade, to eliminate the system of quota protection on textiles known as the Multifiber Agreement (MFA), and to extend the trading rules to cover services, intellectual property, and trade-related investment measures.[13] They also founded a world trade organization with enhanced powers to settle disputes and monitor the trading practices of its members. As of 1994, the WTO had expanded to include more than 120 nations, with formerly planned economies such as China and the Russian Federation and many developing countries eagerly seeking to join.

The multilateral system has also had its problems. As the focus has shifted away from the relatively easy task of reducing barriers protecting industrial products, achieving agreement has become more difficult. The Uruguay Round negotiations were lengthy and complex. In many important areas, such as services and agricultural, liberalization has remained fairly limited. Moreover, considerable controversy exists over whether additional agreements are needed to govern competition policies, liberalize investment, and establish common standards for labor and the environment.

Preferential trading arrangements (PTAs) have also had a checkered history. To be sure, the rapid growth and liberalization achieved by European countries between 1958 and 1973 coincided with the formation of the European Community (EC) and the European Free Trade Area (EFTA), but regional arrangements

---

12. For a survey see Frankel (1996).
13. For a more complete appraisal see Collins and Bosworth (1994).

were also associated with the disastrous fragmentation of the world economy into trading blocs in the 1930s and with the ill-fated arrangements among developing countries in the 1950s and 1960s.

The agreements among developing countries often failed miserably.[14] This might have been expected given their motivation. They were an extension of domestic import substitution and planning policies to the regional level and were usually proposed to achieve scale economies for protectionist policies. The theory was that participating countries would become more specialized. In practice, however, given the general philosophy of trying to produce everything at home, members tended to give one another access to their markets only in those products they imported from the rest of the world. In other words, the region as a whole became more self-sufficient by maximizing trade diversion.

Not surprisingly such preferential trading agreements failed, especially when countries had similar patterns of specialization so that avoiding competition was almost impossible. However, even when there was scope for specialization, once the extraregional trade was diverted, the benefits from the agreement were exhausted.[15]

New Features

Neither past experience nor traditional trade theory provides an adequate guide to current regional arrangements. The forces driving the current developments differ radically from those driving previous waves of regionalization in this century. Unlike the episode of the 1930s, the current initiatives represent efforts to facilitate their members' participation in the world economy rather than their withdrawal from it. Unlike those in the 1950s and 1960s, the initiatives involving developing countries are part of a strategy to liberalize and open their economies to implement export- and foreign-investment–led policies rather than to promote import substitution.[16]

---

14. See, for example, Hazlewood (1979).
15. See Langhammer (1992).
16. See Oman (1994) for a discussion of the driving forces behind recent regionalization.

Initiatives that begin as efforts at liberalization could evolve in protectionist directions or have other detrimental effects, but the current moves toward regionalization are, by and large, not responses to thwart globalization. On the contrary, they are attempts to meet the needs arising from globalization. Many important regional initiatives are not developing as arrangements in which insiders limit their contacts with outsiders. Instead, they are developing as inclusive arrangements. Members allow outsiders to join or independently join them in developing similar arrangements.

Most theorizing about regionalism considers these arrangements in the context of a traditional paradigm in which trade policy is characterized by changes to barriers at the border. Regional arrangements are modeled either as customs unions (members have free trade internally and a common external tariff) or as free trade areas (internal barriers are eliminated while external tariffs differ). Many of the empirical studies of these arrangements similarly construct models that focus on the effects of lowering tariff and nontariff barriers.[17] But although the removal of internal border barriers is certainly an important feature, focusing only on these barriers overlooks much of what regional arrangements are about. The traditional perspective is at best incomplete and at worst misleading.

In many cases these emerging arrangements are also meant to achieve deeper integration of international competition and investment. Once tariffs are removed, complex problems remain because of differing regulatory policies among nations. Traditionally, such policies are determined and administered at the national level, according foreign goods and firms nondiscriminatory national treatment—an approach I have called shallow integration. Increasingly, however, globalization is creating pressures to reconcile divergent national practices.

Indeed, why assume that the nation-state should alone be responsible for regulatory regimes and other public goods? Some goods and rules are better provided locally, while for others bilateral and plurilateral international arrangements may be appro-

17. For a discussion of these methodologies as applied to NAFTA see Lustig, Bosworth, and Lawrence (1992).

priate. In the national context an extensive theory deals with assigning authority over different aspects of fiscal policy to different levels of government—the literature on fiscal federalism. Tensions between centralization and decentralization are inevitable. On the one hand, to realize scale economies and internalization, the scope of governance should be increased. On the other hand, to realize a more precise matching of tastes and choices and enhance accountability, governance should be localized. Clearly, however, the ideal assignment level will not always be either the nation-state or the world. In some cases, for example, global warming or global financial networks, the appropriate level may be the world; in other cases, the local community assumes authority.

Focusing only on border barriers could miss many of the effects of a deeper regional arrangement. The EU might do nothing to change its external tariffs, but the adoption of a single European product standard, for example, could affect both intra- and extra-European trade flows.

Clarifications

When I talk in this book about deeper integration, that is, integration that moves beyond the removal of border barriers, and contrast it with shallow integration, that is, trade liberalization, I do not mean to imply that deeper is better. Indeed, deeper international integration could be better or worse, depending on the nature of the policies that are harmonized and the countries to which they are applied. Deeper integration could, for example, take the form of imposing measures on countries that are inappropriate for their stage of development—such as excessively stringent environmental standards, or which reduce economic efficiency—such as the Common Agricultural Policy in the European Union. Alternatively, deeper integration could enact measures that enhance efficiency—such as the international enforcement of competition policy—and help match the scope of governance with the problem, such as the international implementation of policies to deal with global greenhouse gases.

In this book I will be referring to regional arrangements, but unless clear from the context, this term includes international economic arrangements among members who are drawn from disparate geographic locations. Indeed, geographic proximity is not necessarily the most important determinant of participation in "regional" arrangements. To be sure, in general neighbors do have a tendency to enjoy closer economic relations, but some other determinants of trade and investment may make distant countries more suitable partners. And neighbors may have similar income levels, cultural, historical, and political traditions and so be more willing to share in arrangements for governance, but again this is not necessarily true. Many neighboring countries mistrust each other, and countries may have more in common with others outside their region.

Chapter 2

Globalization and the Demand for Deeper Integration

CORPORATE LEADERS have strongly supported recent regional agreements. In Europe, the initiative to establish a single market was promoted by large European firms who argued that a fragmented Europe deprived them of the scale economies they needed to be competitive. Similarly, the North American Free Trade Agreement (NAFTA) was boosted by U.S. business both large (as represented by the Business Round Table) and small (the U.S. Chamber of Commerce).[1] Major free trade agreement supporters in Canada were the Business Council on National Issues and the Canadian Manufacturers Association (CMA).[2] Large Mexican industrial groups strongly backed NAFTA. Private foreign investors have led the informal regional integration in Asia. In the Asia-Pacific Economic Cooperation (APEC) forum, political leaders have explicitly institutionalized the role of business by creating an advisory Pacific Business Forum in June 1994. Large and small firms from the eighteen member countries are represented in this forum, which is charged with providing proposals for facilitating trade and investment within the region. Clearly, these arrangements reflect the functional needs of corporations. In this chapter I explore why.

1. See Fishlow and Haggard (1992).
2. See Doern and Tomlin (1991)

Developed Countries

In the 1950s the United States dominated the world economy.[3] In 1950 it accounted for almost half the world's output, and U.S. living standards were more than twice as high as those in Europe and six times as high as those in Japan. The ingredients in the superior U.S. performance included the world's most highly educated labor force, the latest management techniques, the most modern and largest capital stock, and a large internal market. The United States was the center of global innovation, and its trade was marked by a product cycle in which new products and technologies were initially introduced in the United States and later diffused internationally through both trade and direct foreign investment by American firms.[4]

Geopolitics played an important role in U.S. trade policies. The United States sought to establish a market-based capitalist system to contain the expansion of communism. The United States therefore promoted a multilateral approach based on nondiscrimination. In Europe the major political imperative was promoting economic cooperation to prevent another war between Germany and its neighbors. The European Community was the principal response. Other European nations, particularly those with traditions of neutrality, formed the European Free Trade Area, which allowed them to gain from freer trade but to preserve their foreign policy independence.

During the postwar period, however, U.S. dominance eroded, and the developed countries closed most of the gap that had existed between them and the United States. By the early 1980s, many firms from Europe and Japan were the technological equals, and in some cases, superiors of their American counterparts. The product cycle ran in both directions across the Atlantic and the Pacific.

The process of technological convergence was accompanied by a rapid expansion of trade and investment among the developed

3. This section draws heavily on Lawrence (1993).
4. See, for example, Vernon (1966).

countries. The expansion in trade was surprising in the light of traditional explanations for international trade, which stress *differences* in technology and factor endowments as reasons for trade. To be sure, lower trade barriers, declining transportation costs, and improved communications were part of the explanation. But these countries were becoming increasingly similar in technological capacities and capital-labor ratios. A related surprise was that trade did not reflect interindustry specialization. Increasingly, trade involved countries simultaneously exporting and importing the same types of products—so-called intraindustry trade. This trade occurs when firms that develop a product and fill a particular market niche in one country discover markets in other countries that have consumers with similar tastes and incomes. As Elhanan Helpman and Paul Krugman explain, these trade patterns can be understood once scale economies, product differentiation, and tastes for variety are taken into account.[5] The theory also suggests that the potential for intraindustry trade is greatest where the scope for differentiation is greatest, that is, highly sophisticated manufactured goods such as machinery, pharmaceuticals, and instruments. Indeed, these are precisely the types of products in which developed country exports have increased most rapidly. Direct investment flows frequently reflect skills and know-how. Firms that compete abroad suffer inherent disadvantages. They are less familiar with local conditions than domestic firms, and to offset these disadvantages they must have other intangible assets such as superior technology, patents, or management abilities. The surge of outward foreign investment from the United States into Europe in the 1960s reflected U.S. technological superiority. Similarly, in the 1980s, the increase in foreign investment in the United States by European and Japanese firms and the rise of Japanese foreign investment in Europe underscored the technological and managerial prowess these nations had achieved.

As global competition has intensified, market access has become more important for success. Access for products is crucial because the international diffusion of innovations has become increasingly

5. Helpman and Krugman (1985).

rapid. The diminished time before competitors respond to new innovations makes large global markets essential for spreading the fixed costs of innovation. But the ability to operate abroad has also become vital. Foreign investment and exports have frequently become complementary activities.[6] Firms selling sophisticated products find that a significant local presence can be a prerequisite for marketing, sales, and service. The ability to follow market trends, respond to customer needs, and acquire innovative smaller firms in all major markets has also become important in determining competitive success.

A dramatic rise has occurred in direct foreign investment in service industries. Indeed, foreign investment in services has grown more rapidly than in goods. As manufacturing firms move abroad, other firms providing complementary inputs and services (such as banking, advertising, management consulting) often accompany them.[7] Some of the rise in services for direct foreign investment (FDI) can therefore be understood as complementary to the manufacturing investment. However, independent reasons for the rise also exist. Developments in information technologies have increased global integration in many service sectors that were once isolated. Moreover, in the 1980s, in many economies a strong trend toward financial liberalization, privatization, and deregulation arose, which created investment opportunities in sectors such as banking, communications, utilities, and transportation. In these sectors investment opportunities for foreigners were once relatively limited.[8]

Developing Countries

After the oil shock of 1973, global economic growth slowed down dramatically. Yet a group of Asian developing countries

6. See Encarnation (1992) for a study along these lines.

7. The second half of the 1980s, in particular, were marked by a massive increase in direct foreign investment that was initially concentrated in the developed economies. According to the United Nations, between 1983 and 1989 the dollar value of FDI outflows grew 28.9 percent annually, three times as rapidly as the 9.4 percent pace of world exports and 7.8 percent rate of world GDP. See UN Centre for Transnational Corporations (UNCTNC) (1991, p. 4).

8. See O'Brien (1992).

(Hong Kong, Korea, Singapore, and Taiwan) was able not only to sustain growth but to do so in an outwardly oriented fashion. In an era in which natural resources and primary commodity prices soared, it was, paradoxically, these poorly endowed nations in Asia that outperformed the rest.

At the start of the 1980s, however, with these few noteworthy Asian exceptions, most developing countries had policies that were biased against exports and aimed at import substitution and restricting direct foreign investment. Starting in the mid-1980s, developing nations responded to success and to failure by moving toward liberalization and an outward orientation.[9] Success led to external pressures on Taiwan and Korea to liberalize. Elsewhere, however, shifts toward freer trade and policies encouraging foreign investment were induced by factors such as debt problems, declining commodity prices, the collapse of communism, the Asian example, the encouragement of the International Monetary Fund and World Bank, and the need to attract new capital in new forms.[10]

Today, for example, almost all Latin American nations are committed to open or relatively open trading policies. This pervasive shift toward more liberal trade policies throughout the continent is a striking and remarkable change. Individual country policies have varied, but typical measures included devaluation, relaxation of foreign exchange controls, elimination of import controls, adoption of relatively uniform tariffs, and elimination of export controls taxes and subsidies. As late as 1984 most economies in the region had closed and controlled trade regimes. Indeed, the model of state-led industrialization and import substitution was synonymous with the region.

In the economies in transition, shifts toward open trade policies have also been widespread. As judged by the IMF in 1990, only Poland had an open trade regime, while thirteen other former

9. For more complete accounts see Haggard (1995); Krueger (1995a); Sachs and Warner (1995).

10. According to the 1992 World Investment Report of the United Nations, in 1991, for example, of eighty-two policy changes relating to foreign investment made by thirty-five countries, eighty were intended to ease the process. In seventy countries, privatization programs are offering new opportunities for FDI. See UN Transnational Corporations (1992).

communist countries in Eastern Europe and elsewhere were classified as restrictive.[11] By the end of 1993, only four were still restrictive, with seven classified as moderately restrictive and three as open. The Baltic countries and almost all Eastern European countries were largely free of the quantitative restrictions on imports and exports that had characterized their regimes just a few years earlier.

As in Latin America, Eastern Europe, and Asia, since the mid-1980s African nations have also been shifting toward more liberal trade regimes. Côte d'Ivoire, Gambia, Ghana, Kenya, and Zaire are on the list of liberalizers who have taken some measures to reduce quantitative restrictions, including the allocation of foreign exchange. In general, however, these measures have been less sustained and extensive than elsewhere.

Although these shifts are pervasive and impressive, it should not be assumed that many developing countries can yet be classified as open. Trade reform is typically not achieved overnight and is often marked by policy reversals.[12]

As they seek to attract capital and at the same time pursue programs based on export-led growth, foreign firms become more attractive to developing countries. They bring knowledge about the latest technologies and ready-made access to major markets. Moreover, in many developing countries, accompanying the shift toward more open trade policies has been a reduction in the role of the state through privatization. In this context, foreign investors have become increasingly attractive as providers of capital, technology, and operational skills.

The demand for foreign investment emanating from the developing countries has corresponded with an increased supply from multinational corporations. As international competition intensifies, small cost advantages may have large consequences. Particular national locations are not necessarily well suited for the

---

11. IMF (1994, p. 37). For a more extensive treatment see Bosworth and Ofer (1995).

12. Between 1990 and 1993 of the fifty-nine countries with adjustment programs supported by the IMF, the number classified as having restrictive trade regimes fell from fifty-three to thirty-three, while the number classified as open increased from one to four. IMF (1994, p. 37).

complete manufacture of complex products. With improvements in communications and transportation, firms are able to produce products by sourcing from multiple locations. Raw materials might best be sourced in one country, labor-intensive processes performed in a second, and technologically sophisticated processes in a third. Multinationals from many nations are therefore expanding their foreign investments.

Traditionally, foreign direct investment in developing countries occurred to gain access to raw materials. Later, in countries following protectionist import-substitution policies, investors were attracted by the prospects of selling behind trade barriers in a large internal market.[13] Although the motive of an attractive domestic market persists, as developing countries have lowered their trade barriers, investment has increasingly been motivated toward servicing export markets.[14] Those able to offer export platforms have become most successful in attracting FDI.[15]

Implications

The increased importance of international investment naturally shifts attention from trade to investment barriers. Attention becomes focused on national differences in the ease with which foreign firms can enter new markets through both acquisition and new establishment. The effects of domestic regulations and taxes on the conditions under which such firms can operate are also highlighted. Similarly, firms who plan to source in one country and sell in others need security about the rules and mechanisms governing trade. Such firms also prefer secure

13. In the 1970s, therefore, the developing countries receiving the largest foreign investment flows were Brazil (1.3 billion annual average inflow), Mexico (0.6 billion), Malaysia (0.3), Nigeria (0.3), Singapore (0.3), and Egypt (0.3). Of these only Singapore was an open, export-oriented economy. UN Transnational Corporations (1992, p. 317).

14. See Wells (1992).

15. Between 1980 and 1990, the list of developing economies receiving the largest annual average inflows of FDI is headed by Singapore ($2.3 billion), followed by Mexico (1.9), Brazil (1.8), China (1.7), Hong Kong (1.1), and Malaysia (1.1). Of these only Brazil has not emphasized export-oriented investment. UN Transnational Corporations (1992, p. 237).

intellectual property rights and technical standards and regulations that are compatible.

For developing countries, especially those previously inhospitable toward foreign investment, establishing the credibility of new policies to attract investment and securing access to markets for exports become imperative. For some developing countries, "importing" new institutions and regulatory systems may be easier than developing them independently. Such institutions may not match domestic conditions precisely, but they have been pretested in the international arena and are compatible with its norms. For nations in Eastern Europe, for example, adopting policies that conform to EU norms is attractive. Finally, entering international negotiations can affect an internal debate. Often, domestic forces interested in liberalization will find their hand strengthened if they can present their policies as part of an international liberalization agreement.[16]

Deeper Integration

Given these developments, the reasons for the distinctive character of the emerging regional arrangements become clearer. They are motivated by the desire to facilitate international investment and the operations of multinational firms as much as the desire to promote trade. Although liberalization to permit trade requires the removal of border barriers—a relatively shallow form of integration—the development of regional production systems and the promotion of service investment require deeper forms of international integration, for example, the elimination of differences in national production and product standards that make regionally integrated production costly. Investment also depends on credible and stable governance mechanisms and secure access to large foreign markets unhindered by customs officials or by domestic actions such as antidumping. Since much of the investment relates to the provision of services, the regulatory regimes governing establishment and operation become the focus of attention.

16. See, for example, Haggard (1995).

These developments have, to be sure, affected the multilateral trade agenda. The Uruguay Round, for example, included agreements that limited trade-related investment measures such as the use of provisions for local content and export requirements, placed disciplines on the use of standards, required enforcement of intellectual property rights, liberalized trade in services, clarified the rules on antidumping and subsidies, and established a more binding mechanism for the resolution of disputes.

Opponents

The emphasis on investment and the deeper nature of these agreements also explains some of the political opposition to which these agreements have given rise. It is well known that mobile factors can escape taxation. As capital becomes more mobile and competition to attract capital intensifies, the ability to impose taxes and other measures that raise costs are reduced. Accordingly, proponents of tougher regulatory measures for labor and the environment feel threatened by international agreements that facilitate such mobility. These groups basically have two responses. They can oppose such agreements, or they can try to establish common rules as part of the agreement. The venomous debates in the United States about NAFTA, and in Canada about the U.S.-Canada Free Trade Agreement, reflected the power of this opposition to an agreement they felt gave greater weight to corporate interests than to their concerns about labor standards and environmental and consumer-safety regulations. In Europe, the social charter is an example of how groups seeking to advance the welfare state can use regionalism to achieve their goals.

Others worry about the erosion in national sovereignty represented by these arrangements. Given the deeper nature of these agreements, these concerns are to be expected. In Europe, this anxiety is expressed in fears about the "democratic deficit," when decisions are made by distant bureaucrats in Brussels rather than local citizens; in the United States, by opposition to NAFTA and the WTO.

The Corporate Role

The hope is that regional agreements will move countries toward economic integration that is deeper than that currently feasible under GATT. The concern is that under the influence of companies new systems of rules will be set to help insiders and hurt outsiders. Skeptics such as Anne Krueger, Bernard Hoekman, and Raymond Vernon fear that while new regional agreements masquerade as free trade agreements, they have been severely compromised by intricate rules of origin and other loopholes that may represent a retreat from freer trade rather than a movement toward it.[17]

Does the strong role by corporations in influencing trade policies promote multilateral liberalization as well as regional liberalization? Analysts are divided. Some argue multinationals care more about investment access than open trade. When it comes to border barriers such as tariffs, Louis Wells argues that multinationals may have a strong interest in regional liberalization but a weaker interest in global liberalization. Wells suggests that because the production operations of U.S. multinationals are regionally self-contained, they are fairly insensitive to trade barriers around the region. By contrast, he notes that key functions such as research and development and finance and marketing can be executed globally, despite trade barriers. Raymond Vernon by contrast suggests that regionalization is simply a halfway step in the process of globalization. As such, firms will begin regionally but ultimately depend on global markets. Initiatives for regional integration will be followed by multilateral ones.

Trade Patterns

During the postwar period almost all economies have become more dependent on trade. Some data suggest an intensification in the share of intraregional trade in the second half of the 1980s in the EC and Southeast Asia and a shift toward increased reliance by Latin America on trade with North America during the 1980s.

17. See Hoekman (1992); Krueger (1993b); Vernon (1994).

Importantly, however, over longer periods no clear trends toward increased reliance on intraregional trade have emerged; increased shares of intraregional trade do not necessarily indicate greater barriers to extraregional trade.

The importance of extraregional trade can also be usefully measured by the ratio of total extraregional trade—exports plus imports—to GNP. Extraregional trade is clearly very significant to North America, especially to the United States. Since goods output accounts for about 40 percent of GDP in North America, this share implies that about 25 percent of sales of goods in North America involve a buyer or a seller from outside the region. Although west European extraregional trade is far smaller than intraregional trade, measured as a share of GDP, extraregional trade is more important to Europe than to North America. In sum, the importance of extraregional trade to nations all over the world means that no region is in a position to sever its trade ties with the rest of the world by forming closed blocs.

Chapter 3

The Impact of
Regional Arrangements

R EGIONAL INTERNATIONAL economic arrangements take a variety
of forms as nations move progressively toward deeper economic integration. *Free trade areas* eliminate internal tariff and
nontariff trade barriers but do not harmonize external barriers.
Customs unions remove internal barriers and establish a common
external tariff. *Common markets* are customs unions in which barriers to the mobility of labor and capital are eliminated. Countries
can also cooperate to establish a common currency and common
economic policies, establishing an *economic and monetary union.*
Finally nations can form a single state in a *confederation.*

Several major regional arrangements have emerged over the past
decade with some of these features. Clearly, the European Union
has moved far beyond a common market and progressively deepened its relationships under the single European Act and the
Maastricht Treaty, which envisages full economic and monetary
union for participants by 2000. The North American Free Trade
Agreement (NAFTA) is usually called a free trade agreement—
nations do not have a common external tariff—but it also establishes free movement for capital (although not for labor) and
includes arrangements for international cooperation on issues such
as oversight of antidumping and countervailing duty actions, and
side agreements on labor standards and environment. The precise
nature of the Asia-Pacific Economic Cooperation (APEC) forum
has yet to be established, but participants have committed themselves to an agenda that covers not only trade liberalization but

also measures for trade facilitation (agreement on competition policy, standards, foreign investment, customs procedures, and regulatory policies) and economic cooperation (technical assistance and aid).

To fully appraise these more recent arrangements, analysis that uses the traditional customs union theory clearly needs to be supplemented.

Customs Union and the Theory of the Second Best

International trade theory states that in a competitive global economy, complete free trade will maximize global welfare. However, the verdict is more ambiguous on the welfare implications of a preferential trade agreement that removes the barriers between only a few trading partners.

Superficially, it seems plausible that if free trade is optimal for the world, any movement toward free trade will improve global welfare. Removing the trade barriers within a group of countries without raising barriers to other trading partners seems to be a step in the right direction. However, theory has demonstrated that such measures do not necessarily make the world better off and do not even necessarily make those concluding such agreements better off.

If trade barriers were the only market imperfection in the world, their elimination would improve aggregate welfare. However, if not all barriers are removed, or if other market imperfections besides trade barriers exist, one cannot be sure that removing some barriers will be welfare improving. The reason is that in a world in which market imperfections remain after the trade barrier has been removed, prices will not reflect social opportunity costs. Resources could therefore shift away from rather than toward their optimal allocation.

The possibility that aggregate global welfare can be damaged even though the world as a whole is moved closer to free trade is a startling result with more general implications. Thinking about the example of preferential trading agreements led Richard G. Lipsey and Kelvin Lancaster to enunciate the "general theory of second best," which states that reducing some distortions while others remain in place does not necessarily increase welfare.[1] If it is impossible to satisfy all the optimum conditions (in this case, global free trade), then a change that brings about the satisfaction of some of the optimum conditions (in this case a free trade area) may make things better or worse. As Jacob Viner emphasized, eliminating the internal trade barriers in a customs union will lead to more trade among the partners, and this "trade creation" should add to welfare. *But a customs union could also reduce trade between the members and the rest of the world.* This "trade diversion" could misallocate global resources. If outside producers are more efficient than those inside the agreement, global efficiency declines when the producers within the agreement expand production and the producers in the rest of the world contract production.[2]

The following example illustrates this argument. Assume that prior to implementing a free trade agreement with the United States, all television sets purchased in Mexico are subject to a tariff of 10 percent. Assume that Japan produces TVs under competitive conditions, which it sells at a cost of $100, but the United States could only produce such sets at $105. Initially, all TVs sold in Mexico and elsewhere would be Japanese. These would be imported at a price of $100 from Japan and sold to Mexican consumers for $110, with the additional $10 representing the tariff that would be paid by Mexican consumers to the Mexican government. Assume now that a free trade agreement is signed between the United States and Mexico, which removes tariffs between Mexico and the United States but retains Mexico's tariffs on other countries. Mexican consumers will now have a choice between buying American TVs, which will sell in Mexico at $105, or Japanese TVs, which will sell at $110. They will buy U.S. TVs and be better off. However, the Mexican economy as a whole will be worse off. Before the agreement, Mexico bought TVs from Japan. Although consumers paid $110, $10 was just a transfer from Mexican consum-

1. Lipsey and Lancaster (1956).
2. Viner's original presentation of this theory was couched purely in terms of the costs of production. As Meade (1955) and Lipsey (1957) later pointed out, the removal of tariffs also brings a benefit from less distorted consumption. Thus welfare in an FTA member *could* rise, even though it is buying from a higher cost source, if the benefits from more efficient consumption exceed the loss of tariff revenues.

ers to the Mexican government. The economy as a whole, therefore, spent only $100 per TV. After the agreement, however, Mexico is spending $105 per TV. TV prices in Mexico do not reflect their social opportunity costs. The impact of the agreement is to expand TV production in the United States, which is relatively less efficient, and to reduce it in Japan, which is relatively more efficient.[3]

Of course, not all of the increased trade between partners will represent expansion from a less efficient source. Pure trade creation could also result. Assume in the example that initially Mexico could produce TV sets for $107. In this case, prior to the agreement Mexico would not have imported them from Japan, instead it would have supplied these TV sets domestically. In this case, Mexico would benefit from the agreement, which would allow it pay only $105 per TV, although of course it would have done even better by liberalizing fully and buying the sets from Japan.[4]

Implications

The theory of the second best implies that the rapid growth in the internal trade between members of a customs union does not necessarily mean the union's welfare is being enhanced. Naturally this insight leads to the prescription that only those free trade agreements that are net trade creating should be concluded.[5] And

3. Cooper and Massell (1965) point out, in this example, that instead of forming a customs union, Mexico could achieve higher welfare (the same levels of production and consumption with more government revenue) by imposing a nondiscriminatory import tariff equal to two dollars. See, however, Wonnacott and Wonnacott (1981).

4. The results obtained here are sensitive to the assumptions made. Corden (1972) shows that scale economies complicate the analysis. In addition to the traditional trade creation and trade diversion there can also be trade suppression and cost reduction effects. The former occurs when, as a result of access to a larger market, a producer expands and thus displaces goods that would have been imported. This is not necessarily efficient, since if it was, it would have occurred prior to the union. However, there could also be cost reductions, which do raise efficiency.

5. Most theorizing about preferential trade agreements assumed that nations sought to maximize their overall welfare. Increasingly, however, more attention has been paid to the distributional effects of trade policy. Under such circumstances, Grossman and Helpman (1993) have found in a median voter model that free trade areas are most likely to be supported when trade diversion outweighs trade creation. This is precisely the case when these agreements are harmful.

thus economists generalize about the countries best suited to form preferential trading arrangements or about rules that would offset some of the negative effects of these agreements.

Natural Trading Partners

In the abstract, trade creation will be largest when partners in a preferential trade agreement (PTA) initially have high levels of protection that suppress their trade, and when both partners produce many goods prior to the PTA, but only one of them would produce the goods under conditions of free trade between them. Sometimes these countries are described as "actually competitive" but "potentially complementary." Trade diversion, however, will be smallest when participating countries have low levels of trade with the rest of the world or when their trade with the rest of the world is not competitive with that of nations joining the agreement.

The literature has searched for rules that would indicate, presumptively, partners for whom PTAs would raise welfare. These have included regional partners—since geographic proximity generally promotes trade, trade creation could be large; partners at similar stages of development—since intraindustry trade flourishes between developed countries; and large PTAs—since the more varied the membership, the greater the opportunities for specialization.[6] Importantly, geographic proximity need not be the dominant consideration in selecting ideal partners for preferential arrangements. Indeed, countries from different regions may make better partners than those from the same region. Furthermore, the theory does not produce rules that are foolproof. Indeed, it suggests that it is dangerous to try to rely on such generalizations as if they provide completely dependable guides to the likely extent of net trade creation. There are no hard and fast rules and thus no substitute for a case-by-case empirical analysis.

6. For discussion of the role of transport costs see Krugman (1991b) and Frankel, Stein, and Wei (1993). For a discussion of size see Deardorf and Stern (1991) and Krugman (1991a).

Outsiders

Theory does suggest, however, that trading partners who do not participate in a preferential arrangement will be hurt even when global welfare as a whole is enhanced.[7] Unless the outsiders are too large (or the preferential trading area too small) for the arrangement to affect world prices, outsiders as a whole will be harmed because their terms of trade are likely to deteriorate as a result of the trade diversion.[8] But again exceptions could occur. If the internal trade liberalization has dynamic effects that increase growth, or if there are scale economies that stimulate the demand for imports from outside the region, the income effects of liberalization could more than offset trade diversion, thereby raising outside welfare.[9]

Compensation

The damaging effects of the preferential agreement on outsiders come from trade diversion. If preferential arrangements hurt outsiders and benefit those concluding the arrangement, it might be possible to offset the damage done to outsiders, and leave no one worse off. M. C. Kemp and H. Y. Wan have shown that the key to making sure that preferential arrangements do not reduce global welfare is to offset this damage by keeping the trade flows of the rest of the world unchanged.[10] This result can be achieved by lowering the external tariffs of agreement members to maintain their trade flows with the rest of the world at the same time as the agreement is implemented. Since the effects of trade diversion would be eliminated, all that is left is trade creation and thus the world as a whole must be better off. In this sense, to form a

---

7. Mundell (1964).

8. If the intraunion terms of trade are changed, Corden gives an example in which the outsiders' terms of trade can actually improve. Corden (1984, p. 120). "If C [the outsider] imports 1 and 2 from the union, and the relative prices of 1 and 2 change, the terms of trade measured in terms of goods 3 (C's export) might improve in terms of 1 but worsen in terms of 2. Because of intra-union terms of trade changes, . . . C's terms of trade could thus improve."

9. See, for example, Baldwin (1989).

10. See Kemp and Wan (1976).

customs union is to move unambiguously in the direction of free trade.

Additional Liberalization

Free trade opponents of preferential trading agreements assume that in the absence of regional free trade agreements, multilateral liberalization will take place. However, in some cases it may be possible to liberalize in a free trade area when it is not possible to do so unilaterally or multilaterally.

It is generally agreed that because firms can act collectively more easily, they are more powerful politically than consumers. This makes import liberalization politically difficult because even when the country as a whole will gain, the benefits will be enjoyed by consumers in the form of lower prices while the costs will be borne by those firms who compete with imports. If consumers are poorly organized, import-competing firms lobbying for protection might have the upper hand. To offset this advantage, it might be necessary to have another group of producers—namely, exporters—also supporting liberalization.

Indeed, exporting firms generally support liberalization. Economic theory says that letting in more imports will stimulate exports through a variety of channels. First, increased imports could lower the exchange rate and thus promote exports. Second, the availability of cheap imported inputs could improve exporter competitiveness, and third, if resources are freed up from import activities, they will be free for use in export industries. But these arguments are very subtle, and the effects operate through indirect channels that are not readily appreciated. Thus unilateral liberalization is politically difficult, even when it is economically beneficial.

But liberalization by participating in multilateral negotiations is not especially attractive to exporting interests originating in small countries. The offers of other nations are not likely to be influenced by the liberalization in a single country. Thus particularly in a system such as GATT in which all members are given most favored nation treatment unconditionally, exporters will find it difficult to see lobbying for domestic liberalization as worthwhile.

Moreover, since GATT has operated on the principle of special and differential treatment for developing countries, exporters from small developing countries have even less reason to promote domestic liberalization. This tendency toward free riding creates problems for exporters from large countries. These considerations are different in preferential trading agreements. Exporters will see gains in the form of more open foreign markets that are contingent on domestic liberalization, and therefore they are likely to lobby more enthusiastically for such agreements.[11]

If scale economies are important, the benefits from liberalization may be greater for small countries than for large countries. Accordingly, the bargaining power of large countries may be greater in such negotiations. Indeed, Jagdish Bhagwati and others argue that this power can lead to undesirable demands being placed on small countries.[12] Large countries may be able to obtain policy concessions in areas besides trade when negotiating such agreements. But countries are not forced to negotiate such agreements. Presumably they do so because they believe it makes them better off. Indeed, historically the chief obstacle to a North America Free Trade Agreement was concern in Canada and Mexico about U.S. domination. But apparently, the cost-benefit calculations have shifted.

Deeper Integration and Regional Arrangements

But what does theory say if regional arrangements cover policies that are not dealt with by GATT?

Beyond GATT?

The postwar rules for international trade that are enshrined in GATT have evolved to reflect a world of sovereign nation-states, each with its own domestic policies and institutions. These rules have been designed to achieve freer trade by lowering tariff barriers

---

11. The same would be true for multilateral liberalization if it was made conditional rather than unconditional.

12. Bhagwati and Krueger (1995).

while simultaneously retaining national sovereignty. GATT has tried to eliminate the discriminatory treatment of foreign goods, but it has not tried to harmonize domestic policies and has concentrated on only those aspects of regulatory and institutional behavior that clearly distort or hinder trade. With the exception of recent efforts in the Uruguay Round to devise global standards for intellectual property, GATT has tried, whenever possible, to avoid the problems of reconciling or harmonizing different national policies. GATT has also relied heavily on the voluntary compliance of members to its rules and only recently has the World Trade Organization been provided with a dispute settlement procedure with more teeth.

Beyond Trade

Traditional trade theory has also largely ignored the existence of different national institutions. Trade policy is generally modeled as decisions to change border barriers while other governmental policies are usually ignored. One justification is that these differences can simply be subsumed as similar to differences in technology or climate. In fact, the paradigms of traditional theory and the GATT notion of sovereign national states fit quite neatly with each other provided that institutions (and regulations) can be taken as given.

In traditional analysis, therefore, the dominant goal is the maximization of global welfare by multilateral free trade. Each nation exploits its distinctive features by freely trading with the rest of the world. Against this paradigm, preferential free trade arrangements are judged to be "second best."

However, there is a different perspective on these questions, which does not simply assume that the nation-state is always the most appropriate unit of jurisdiction and decision-making power. This perspective leads one to ask, what level of organization is the most appropriate to provide public goods and regulatory regimes?

The degree of integration needed to maximize public welfare will reflect two considerations: the technology of producing public services and customer choice. The benefits and costs of different public goods and externalities will be realized on a variety of spatial scales. Purely private goods should be provided through decentralized markets. Other goods generate local externalities and should be provided by local governments. In still other cases, the externalities will span larger areas. Some goods are public, in the sense that consumption is *nonrival*. For example, an individual can obtain knowledge without detracting from the knowledge of others. Goods such as knowledge may be provided locally, nationally, or internationally, depending on the span of public-ness—the domain within which additional consumers can costlessly enjoy these goods. The mobility of factors and consumers dramatically complicates the ability of local authorities to internalize the costs and benefits of providing public goods.

Finally, if the tastes of consumers vary widely, it is efficient to accommodate such variations even when some advantages in production efficiency might be gained from a broad governmental authority.

Naturally, as global interdependence increases, so too do the pressures for common rules and institutions at supranational levels. At the same time, however, as incomes increase, the scope for exercising different preferences also increases.[13] It is no surprise, therefore, that as regional arrangements challenge the sovereignty of the nation-state, it has also come under attack in many parts of the world by pressure from separatist movements and others demanding increased subnational autonomy. Supranational and subnational regionalism are both responses to the diminished role of the nation-state as a provider of public goods.

First or Second Best?

In principle, the regional (or plurilateral) arrangements found in deeper integration need not be second best, they could be the first best. As mentioned earlier, some activities may best be carried out on a global level, others on a plurilateral level, and some may best be left to the subnational level.

Take currency as an example. One extensive theory suggest that under some conditions neither the nation-state nor the world is the

13. See Casella (1993).

optimal area to provide currency.[14] Although a single global currency would clearly economize on transaction costs, individual nations would also lose their ability to apply monetary policies independently. Accordingly a global currency might not be first best. However, for small nations that are very open to trade or labor migration, the ability to use monetary policy and exchange rate changes may be quite limited, and thus the benefits of a separate national currency might be small. In principle, therefore, an arrangement with several multinational currency groupings might be better than either national currencies or a single global currency.[15]

Intellectual property rights is another example.[16] The removal of trade barriers occurs under the presumption that both countries have something to gain from liberalization. By contrast, in the case of intellectual property, countries that do not innovate may simply lose.[17] The absence of intellectual property rights allows citizens to copy innovations performed elsewhere without offering compensation to the originator. Once an agreement is enforced, however, beneficiaries must pay royalties. Whether such an agreement makes the world better off is an empirical question. On the one hand, more innovation is encouraged, on the other, the use of such inventions is made more expensive.

Recognizing the deeper nature of these agreements provides important challenges for modeling their effects. Indeed these challenges have not been adequately met.[18] For example, uncertainty about property rights and market access could have a powerful impact on resource allocation and investment. A regional agreement that guaranteed domestic firms better access to large neighboring markets and foreign investors more secure control could boost investment and give rise to important dynamic gains. Indeed a key Mexican motive for NAFTA was to ensure that its economic reform policies would be credible and permanent. But modeling

14. The classic references are McKinnon (1963); Mundell (1961).
15. See Bryant (1995) and Eichengreen (1995) for further discussion.
16. See, for example, Deardorff (1993).
17. Bhagwati (1994a).
18. For further discussion see Lustig, Bosworth, and Lawrence (1992).

such a process is not easy, and it is usually easier to estimate the impact of changes in tariffs and other prices than to gauge the effect of changes in rules.

The deeper nature of regional agreements also complicates the appraisal of their effects on welfare. For instance, the normal presumptions about trade creation and diversion may not hold. It is often presumed, for example, that preferential trading arrangements will reduce exports from outside the region. However, regional agreements that go beyond trade barriers could actually stimulate such trade. For example, if members agree on tougher pollution controls or labor standards, their imports of products from nations with more lenient standards could rise. Similarly, the adoption of a common standard in the regional arrangement may make it less costly not only for domestic producers but also for producers outside the region to sell their products. The adoption of constraints on national state aids would also provide benefits for both internal and external producers who compete with firms that might once have received such subsidies, and tougher antitrust enforcement could provide improved market access for both internal and external producers.

In empirical studies, a reduction in external trade is often an indication of trade diversion—that is, a member of an agreement is buying products from a less efficient internal source. However, deeper agreements could make regional firms more efficient. This result might lead to a reduction of external trade, but it would not represent trade diversion that reduced welfare. For example, changes in domestic regulations could give internal firms cost advantages over outsiders that resulted both in fewer imports from outside the region and in lower internal costs. This, as I argue later, has important implications for proposals that outsiders should be compensated for their loss of trading opportunities when preferential trading arrangements are formed.

Possibly, however, even without raising border barriers or increasing internal trade, deeper regional agreements could become more closed to outsiders. For instance, adoption of a common standard might discriminate against external imports and raise internal costs. Or adoption in the region as a whole of common cartel-like industrial policies could limit the access of external producers.

As these examples indicate, from an efficiency standpoint, deeper international agreements could be better or worse than the domestic policies they replace or discipline. *Deeper does not necessarily mean better or more efficient.* First, the choice of the level of government is a matter of judgment and depends on balancing the costs and benefits of more centralized government. Mistakes could be made, and policies implemented by international agreement could violate the principle of subsidiarity. Second, much depends on the policies adopted. Harmonizing on the wrong policy could be worse than retaining national policies that are not linked.

In sum, although traditional trade theory offers interesting insights into the benefits and costs of regional arrangements and their dynamics, the deeper aspects of these agreements mean they must be viewed through more than the narrow prism of conventional trade theory. Furthermore, the many considerations that will affect outcomes suggest that there is no substitute for considering specific historical experiences.

Chapter 4

System Dynamics

D O PREFERENTIAL arrangements lead to more or less trade liberalization? Viewed statically, on the basis of removing barriers at the border, preferential trading arrangements are inferior to multilateral free trade. But they can also be viewed dynamically, as measures that move the world toward global free trade. Indeed, during the postwar period the world has moved toward free trade partly in a series of GATT trade rounds that have successively lowered trade barriers and partly through preferential arrangements. One process of liberalization entails partial liberalization but full participation; the other, full liberalization but partial participation. Whether the rise of preferential trading arrangements makes the achievement of full multilateral liberalization more or less likely is an important and yet unanswered question.

In general, economic liberalization will reflect interests and power. It will depend on the incentives of the actors who can influence policy on the one hand, and their ability to influence policy on the other. To derive conclusions one must model the process by which trade policy is made. Some models assume countries behave as rational unitary actors, others explicitly model the internal policy-economy of national decisionmaking. Some assume countries undertake these decisions in a global system in which there are no rules, others consider the role of different rules and regimes. Each approach yields insights, although none seems to yield definitive answers.

The literature provides some reasons that could tilt policies toward further liberalization and others that could tilt them toward further protection.[1] As might be expected, predictions are sensitive to how the dynamics of trade liberalization are modeled, whether the arrangements considered are customs unions or free trade areas (although there is no firm presumption that one particular type is more liberal), and the rules of the international trading system.

Market Power

When small countries impose trade barriers, they simply hurt themselves by distorting domestic production and consumption. If their policies were focused only on maximizing efficiency, once they realized the damage inflicted by trade barriers, they should remove them unilaterally. Taking the actions of others as given, for small countries, unilateral liberalization will be superior to entering customs unions, because the latter may involve trade diversion whereas full liberalization will not.[2]

But the incentives for protection in a large country are different. By discouraging imports, a tariff could lower the world price of imports. And since fewer exports would be sold to pay for imports, a smaller supply of export products on world markets could raise the price of export goods. For large countries, therefore, tariffs have two offsetting effects. They reduce welfare by distorting production and consumption, and they increase welfare by improving the terms of trade (the ratio of export to import prices). The tariff that maximizes the difference between these effects is known as the optimal tariff.[3] Therefore, taking the tariff levels in the rest of the world as given—an important assumption—a large country concerned only with national welfare can restrict its trade to take advantage of its monopoly or monopsony power by imposing an optimal tariff.

1. See Frankel (1996) for a more complete survey.
2. The real advantage to such countries from GATT is the ability to benefit from liberalization by large countries.
3. See Johnson (1958); Johnson (1987).

Theory also suggests that the tariff will be positively related to the size of the country. An increase in the relative size of a customs union would raise its optimal tariff.[4] Consequently, once a block is formed, as a whole it may be better off with some form of tariff than with complete free trade.[5] This line of argument suggests that the formation of regional arrangements will weaken the incentives for multilateral liberalization.

But there are reasons to question this conclusion. In practice, the optimal tariff argument has been a poor guide to policy. The most liberal trading systems have emerged when the world was dominated by a single hegemonic economy, such as the United Kingdom in the midnineteenth century and the United States in the midtwentieth century. Yet this arrangement was precisely the regime under which one might have expected an optimal tariff to prevail.

The naive application of the optimal tariff argument ignores the possibility of retaliation. Large actors cannot overlook the effects of their actions on the system as a whole. It is true that if there is just one large block, it could find an optimal tariff tempting. But in a system with other large players, individual blocks might be wary of setting off retaliation that could make them all worse off.[6]

Indeed the formation of regional arrangements will not be passively accepted by trading partners. They may respond by demanding offsetting moves toward liberalization or their own accession into the agreement. Moreover, the larger such arrangements, the more likely that such pressure will be brought to bear. Thus the United States was particularly insistent on achieving reductions in the European Community's tariffs immediately after its formation in 1958. (To be sure the EC received reciprocal reductions from its trading partners).[7]

4. See Saxonhouse (1993); Krugman (1991b).

5. Krueger (1993b) expresses the concern that producers benefiting from the rules of origin that result from a free trade area will lobby against their removal and thus make additional liberalization more difficult.

6. Moreover, negotiations between large blocks could be easier because free ridership is less likely and policing easier.

7. Both the EC and EFTA have used international income transfers in connection with adjustments of trade policy. As noted by Kowalczyk and Sjostrom (1993).

The formation of regional arrangements might also give others an increased stake in promoting the multilateral system. As the U.S. response to the European Community indicated, outsiders might also be more willing to liberalize to keep a preferential trading arrangement open (or induce it to liberalize). In the Uruguay Round deliberations, for example, a fear of closed regionalism spurred countries who did not belong to such arrangements to push for a stronger multilateral system.

In some cases, small countries may form customs unions in order to be able to bargain more effectively to obtain liberalization.[8] For example, the Mercosur Common Market composed of Argentina, Brazil, Paraguay, and Uruguay was motivated in part by the desire to bargain more effectively with the United States.

Countries excluded from a preferential agreement may have incentives to join it. If the agreement is open to newcomers, there could be an ever-expanding preferential arrangement that eventually encompasses the world. The incentive to join may increase as an agreement grows and becomes more effective. Richard Baldwin describes this result as the domino effect.[9] He shows how the trade diversion (and the increased efficiency) of countries forming an agreement can raise the costs for other competitors of staying out of it. This occurrence can spur the desire of an excluded country's export firms to join the agreement, thereby spreading the process of liberalization. A key issue under these circumstances is how accession should be granted.

The domino effect Baldwin has identified may well be combined with another that may lead liberalization to spread. By joining several free trade areas, countries that are prepared to liberalize may do so in a piecemeal fashion. Countries benefit from being the hub of a network of free trade agreements. Israel has free trade agreements with the United States and the European Union. Firms exporting from Israel, for example, receive preferential access to both the United States and the European Union. By

8. Indeed this motive may explain why even small countries may do better by forming customs unions than unilaterally moving to free trade. See Wonnacott and Wonnacott (1981).

9. See Baldwin (1993).

contrast, firms in the United States and the European Union receive preferences only in the Israeli market. At the same time, by being open to more than one trading partner, Israel has less trade diversion than it would have compared with having just one such agreement. Ultimately, the best situation for a single small country would be to enjoy preferential access to all markets in the world, while having open borders. If these incentives are present for every country, the system could move to free trade.

Countries trying to achieve this state do face complicated timing decisions. It is necessary to have some preferences remaining to bargain away to achieve access to each new partner, and as countries conclude these agreements, the value of the preferences they confer diminishes. One of the advantages of simultaneous multilateral liberalization is that the incentives to hold back are reduced because countries can keep track of all the concessions they receive in return for the ones they confer.

If full free trade is the outcome, why don't the countries get together and coordinate their actions? Eventually they may, but especially at the start, the first movers gain a temporary advantage because of the preferential access they achieve.

Indeed, a noteworthy aspect of liberalization, particularly in Latin America, has been the tendency of countries to join several free trade areas simultaneously.[10] In the Western Hemisphere, it seems that these areas will now be consolidated into a single free trade area in the Americas.

Capture

Another fear is that insiders in a customs union with a stake in higher protection will capture the decisionmaking process and thus have increased power to thwart liberalization. This concern

10. Between 1990 and 1994, Chile signed free trade agreements with Mexico, Argentina, Bolivia, Venezuela, Colombia, and Ecuador; Mexico signed NAFTA and agreements with Chile, Caricom, Costa Rica, Bolivia, Colombia, and Venezuela; Argentina signed with Brazil, Chile, Bolivia, Venezuela, Ecuador, and the Mercosur customs union with Brazil, Argentina, Paraguay, and Uruguay. Bolivia signed agreements with Uruguay, Argentina, Peru, Chile, and Brazil. Inter-American Development Bank (1995, p. 5).

will be especially pronounced for customs unions where trade policy decisions require unanimity. For example, assume Spain and Poland compete in producing product A. If both were outside the European Union, they would be lobbying the union to lower its tariffs on A. Once Spain achieves access, however, its incentives change, and to preserve its preferential access, it might oppose lower tariffs for Poland.

Moreover, a multilateral system with a few large players could be more susceptible to such footdraggers. For a long time, France opposed agricultural liberalization during the Uruguay Round. Since France was able to affect the position of the European Community as a whole, reaching agreement proved difficult. By contrast, had France been isolated, an arrangement that simply bypassed or excluded France might have been possible.

However, arrangements in a larger customs union may be more difficult to capture than those in single nations because larger groups are more likely to contain countervailing interests. France might oppose agricultural liberalization, but other nations in the European Union did not. Indeed, in the end, France was forced to compromise, partly because of pressures from other members in the union with an interest in agricultural liberalization. Moreover, a customs union such as the European Union has relatively low external tariffs; accession by more protectionist countries makes their tariffs more liberal. This was true for Spain and Portugal, for example, with most of their industrial products.[11]

Political Support

Regional arrangements may raise some alarm because of concern about the diversion of scarce political capital. Trade policymakers who are negotiating and operating regional agreements will have less time and fewer resources available for multilateral negotiations. And perhaps advocates for free trade with particular interests would be satisfied by liberalization with a few key coun-

---

11. In some agricultural products, the United States and other nations demanded compensation.

tries and thus not support multilateral liberalization. The United States is the market Mexican exporters most care about. If the only way the Mexican glass industry could sell in the United States was for the United States to lower its tariffs multilaterally at GATT, Mexican glass exporters might work hard for a GATT agreement. In a coalition with other exporters, they might tilt Mexican support for GATT. If they gained access to the U.S. market through the North American Free Trade Agreement (NAFTA), however, their interest in GATT might subside, and the lobby for multilateral liberalization would be weakened.

However, a regional arrangement might build up the political support for liberalization by accomplishing it gradually rather than all at once. A regional arrangement might reduce the size of import-competing sectors and increase the size of the export sector. This situation could in turn tilt the internal domestic political debate in favor of full liberalization.[12]

System Rules

The rules of the multilateral trading system governing the formation of preferential trading agreements could greatly influence the dynamic path toward full liberalization. Three aspects are important. First, rules for compensation. Do nations forming the agreement have to compensate outsiders? M. C. Kemp and H. Y. Wan, for example, have explored the implications of a compensation rule requiring countries forming a customs union to lower their external tariffs to keep their imports from the rest of the world unchanged. This rule guarantees that all customs union agreements are trade creating. However, in this type of regime countries are stimulated to continuously expand their membership until they reach multilateral free trade. As Kemp and Wan argue, "An incentive to form and enlarge customs unions persists until the world becomes one big customs union, that is until free trade prevails."[13]

12. See Wei and Frankel (1995) for an example.
13. Kemp and Wan (1976, p. 96).

A second rule bears on external protection. GATT has credibly bound the tariff levels of its members and has a set of rules that have provided some discipline on the formation of customs unions and free trade areas. Specifically, GATT requires that such agreements not raise their external tariffs. This rule renders the optimal tariff predictions moot, although such factors could nonetheless affect incentives for additional liberalization. If these disciplines were removed by a breakdown in the GATT system, the dangers of more protectionist reactions would dramatically increase.

The rules for accession, especially about willingness to accept outsiders, are the third crucial aspect of the dynamic development of preferential trading areas. The dynamics of regional groupings that are open to all newcomers will differ from those that retain exclusivity or are selective about who may join. Richard Baldwin explores, for example, how the expansion and deepening of an arrangement will increase the incentive of outsiders with deteriorating competitive positions to seek membership. Sang-Seung Yi shows that if agreements are open to new members, a system of preferential agreements will eventually become a world of full, multilateral free trade.[14]

Customs Unions versus Free Trade Areas

The predictions described above are sensitive according to whether the arrangements are customs unions or free trade areas. Customs unions can remove internal border inspection. But the differential tariff rates that prevail in free trade areas create incentives for arbitrage. Free trade areas must control trade deflection by having rules of origin that prevent importers from bringing in goods through low-duty members and shipping them to countries where duties are higher. This objective requires defining rules and then inspecting *all* goods that cross internal borders in a free trade area to determine whether they qualify for duty-free treatment. In a world where products are increasingly made from components with diverse national sources, this is not easy. Anne Krueger argues

14. Baldwin (1993); Yi (1994).

that these rules of origin can be used as a form of protectionism that then gives domestic firms party to a free trade agreement an incentive to oppose further liberalization.[15] By contrast, she notes such incentives would not exist under customs unions. Therefore, she says, customs union agreements are likely to be less protectionist and, because they create fewer vested interests in protection, probably more amenable to further liberalization.

But some arguments suggest otherwise. Countries in a customs union may have an incentive to increase their protection by exploiting their monopoly power, but in a free trade area, this incentive would be reduced. Indeed, when forming a free trade area, countries can individually reduce their external protection and eliminate the harmful effects of trade diversion.[16] Thus free trade areas might lead to more liberalization than customs unions.

In sum, on the basis of many plausible considerations, one can reach opposite conclusions. On the one hand, naive application of optimal tariffs, dangers of capture by protectionist interests, greater interests in protection, the diversion of political capital and dilution of political support all make multilateral liberalization less likely. On the other hand, reactions by other major players demanding accession or liberalization, the greater ease of monitoring and negotiating, and the increased difficulties of capturing large arrangements all make liberalization more likely. The rules of the game on compensation, protection, and accession can all be important. In the end, there is no substitute, therefore, for seeing which of these effects dominates in practice.

15. Krueger (1993b).

16. Bagwell and Staiger (1993b) find that multilateral trade liberalization is self-reinforcing because of fears of retaliation during the early phases of customs union formation. However, this threat is reduced as the monopoly of the customs union increases. In the case of free trade areas, they show the dynamics are different. Bagwell and Staiger (1993a).

Chapter 5

European Regional Arrangements

THE EUROPEAN UNION, the North American Free Trade Agreement (NAFTA), and the Asia-Pacific Economic Cooperation (APEC) forum can be considered in light of three interrelated questions. First, how deep are these agreements—to what extent do they move beyond dealing with border barriers and how far have they moved beyond GATT in establishing rules for trade and investment? Second, what effect have these agreements had on members and on outsiders? Third, what are the dynamics of these agreements, have they been closed or open, and have they hindered or helped multilateral liberalization?

By signing the Treaty of Rome in 1957, the six original members of the European Economic Community planned to harmonize their tariffs and pursue a common trade policy, that is, a customs union, and to achieve a common market with free movement of goods, services, labor, and capital (the four freedoms). But the EEC was far more than a narrowly economic agreement to achieve a common market. The goals of the Community were political as well as economic.[1] In particular members wanted to enhance economic interdependence so that war between them would be unthinkable. Furthermore, they believed a united Europe would be a bulwark against communism.

---

1. See Wallace (1994) for an excellent analysis of the political dimensions of Europe's integration.

The Treaty of Rome reflects the intention of its signatories to achieve much deeper economic integration than a customs union would. Specifically they seek to harmonize policies toward agriculture, energy, transport, and competition and to engage in fiscal transfers to promote regional development. To achieve these goals, the treaty establishes an elaborate governance structure, which includes the Commission (the administrative and technical body), the Council of Ministers (the primary decisionmaking body), the Court of Justice, and the Assembly (or Parliament).

These governance mechanisms represent significant challenges to national sovereignty because Community members accept the supremacy of Community law over national law in the areas in which the Community has been given competence. Sovereignty among the members is thus shared through these supranational institutions, mechanisms for decisionmaking and enforcement, and a common body of law.

Over time, the Community's power and scope have been enhanced and its goals have become more ambitious, most notably through the Single European Act, signed in 1986, which served as the basis for completing the internal market—the EC 92 program and the Maastricht Treaty, concluded in 1992, which laid out plans for economic and monetary union.

By July 1968, one and a half years ahead of schedule, the EEC had achieved considerable success in eliminating customs duties and quantitative restrictions on intra-EEC trade and in implementing a common external tariff. From 1973 to 1985, the Community broadened its membership as Britain, Denmark, and Ireland joined in the mid-1970s, and Greece, Spain, and Portugal in 1981 and 1986.

Between 1958 and 1973 the EEC enjoyed rapid economic growth. But after 1973 European growth slumped, and in every year between 1973 and 1985 the unemployment rate in the Community increased.[2] One reason given for the slowdown was the exhaustion of the stimulus to internal trade from the removal of internal barriers. Indeed, in the 1970s, the growth in

2. For a more complete analysis of this period see Lawrence and Schultze (1987).

intra-Community trade had slowed.[3] It became apparent that the removal of formal tariffs and many nontariff barriers had not resulted in fully integrated goods markets. Trade was distorted by border inspections, differential taxation, domestic subsidies, discriminatory public procurement, and internal restrictions on market access. Agricultural prices were especially distorted by special so-called green exchange rates. The process of unifying the Community's external trading relations had also not been completed— individual European economies retained a number of sector-specific restrictions on their trade with outsiders. These included voluntary export restraints and minimum price undertakings in sectors such as agriculture, textiles and clothing, automobiles, and consumer electronics.

The Community's piecemeal method of dealing with these barriers, and the unanimity required for any measure to pass, guaranteed that progress toward removing these obstacles would occur at a snail's pace. The Treaty of Rome had promoted freedom of movement for goods, services, labor, and capital, but it did so mainly on the basis of national treatment. It became apparent that by defining standards that were difficult for firms from other European countries to meet, members could simultaneously provide such national treatment and yet discriminate against outsiders. In Germany, for example, the French alcoholic beverage cassis de Dijon could not be sold because it contained insufficient alcohol (17 percent) to meet the German standard for liqueur (32 percent).[4]

To deal more effectively with these issues, in 1985 the European Commission set out in a White Paper a description of the barriers that remained and a timetable for their removal. In July 1987 the Single European Act amended the Treaty of Rome and instituted two key principles that dramatically increased the Community's ability to act. First, instead of unanimity, the principle of qualified majority voting was introduced for most new directives, and sec-

3. Jacquemin and Sapir (1989, p.1).
4. In a famous case, the European Court of Justice set in motion the move toward the widespread application of the mutual recognition principle by ruling that Germany could not maintain a standard that served no public health purpose.

ond, instead of trying to achieve harmonized policies, the principle of mutual recognition in the absence of communitywide standards was explicitly recognized. Under the Single Act those national laws, regulations, and administrative practices that have not been harmonized must be recognized as equivalent. As applied to goods, this principle means that if a product meets the standards required in any of the members, it can be sold in all of them. In other words, the standards of any of the twelve members can be used throughout the community unless minimum community-wide standards have explicitly been set.[5]

The principle of mutual recognition was also used to bolster the rights of establishment for firms and the mobility of labor. Any entity that qualifies to do business in any of the member states can do business in all of them. Thus banks, for example, that are chartered in the United Kingdom can establish branches throughout the European Union, although they remain under U.K. control. Similarly, professionals who are qualified in any country can practice in all. Mutual recognition represents an ingenious solution to the problem that confronts international regulatory harmonization.[6] According to Alan Winters, "The importance of this approach is that it threatens national sovereignty much less directly than does central rule-making."[7] But although the challenge to national sovereignty may not be direct, this practice introduces competition between regulatory regimes within the Community, and this competition—as with other types of competition—requires rules of the game. As Kalypso Nicolaidis has emphasized, acceptance of mutual recognition represents an institutional expression of trust.[8] When countries are willing to accept the regulations of others, they simplify initial negotiations but must exercise considerable tacit understanding of one another.

5. Common EC standards will be limited to areas such as health, safety, the environment, and essential interoperability. Hufbauer (1990, p. 11).

6. Nicolaidis (1989) notes that mutual recognition was used in the Treaty of Rome for professional and educational qualifications, but she argues that its use was confined to this example and applied in a "circumscribed way."

7. Winters (1992, p. 31).

8. Nicolaidis (1989).

The EC 92 program, which aimed at completing the single market by the end of 1992, targeted four types of barriers for elimination. One, fiscal barriers, such as taxes in agriculture and less favorable taxes on firms from other community countries; and quantitative barriers, for example, quotas on production (on steel and agricultural products). Two, limitations on the shares of foreign firms in transportation services and quotas imposed by individual countries against nonmembers (for example, Japanese automobiles). Three, market access restrictions against firms from other Community countries, for example, public procurement, transportation, banking and insurance, and many professions. Four, the costs imposed by borders because of inspection, delays, and differing technical regulations.[9] The White Paper also called for an effective competition policy, and a new merger regulation came into effect in 1990.

Although this initiative to establish a single market was led by members of the Commission in Brussels who were motivated by the goals of political union and stimulating growth, it was also supported by European firms who realized that even fairly large domestic markets such as those of Germany, France, and the United Kingdom were inadequate home bases for global competition.

The Single Market

What was the impact of the EC 92 on its members? Those who have tried to estimate these effects come out with quite different results, depending on how they model the economy and the program.[10] In general, most plausible estimates yield figures that are positive but fairly small.

It is difficult to capture in a model the notion that although the European Community was already a completed customs union, its markets were not fully integrated. Different technical standards,

9. This draws on Flamm (1992, p. 9).

10. The Cecchini report, Cecchini (1988, p. 83), issued by the European Commission claimed that Europe's income would increase between 4.3 and 6.5 percent. However Peck (1989, p. 289) argued that it overstated the microeconomic efficiency to be achieved by a factor of 2 to 3.

border costs, preferential public procurement practices, and other forms of entry barriers, particularly in regulated sectors, all raise costs. One aspect of EC 92 simply involves reducing these costs— which are typically estimated to be around 2 to 3 percent of the value of trade. If trade is 25 percent of income, this amounts to about .5 percent of income. However, such calculations assume a perfectly competitive economy. These remaining impediments allowed firms to exploit their local market power and discriminate among national markets with the result that there were large differences in prices across national markets. Larger effects might be obtained by reducing monopoly power through increasing potential access and thus competitive pressures. Nonetheless, even the models that capture the effects of reducing price-cost distortions because of imperfect competition, exploiting economies of scale, and increasing product diversity suggest benefits that are fairly small. Michael Gasiorek, Alasdair Smith, and Anthony Venables, who aggregate separate industry estimates, arrived at effects equal to 1.5 percent of GDP.[11]

Typically, most general equilibrium models assume a fully employed economy and estimate the effects of EC 92 on improved resource allocation. However, the EC 92 initiative may have also helped spur the entrepreneurial instincts of Europe's business leaders during the strong cyclical recovery in the late 1980s. The EC 92 initiative was successful, not simply in removing barriers but in reorienting the strategies of European firms. Formerly they had considered Europe a set of separate markets, but increasingly they planned their strategies on the assumption of a single market. These strategies were reflected in investment, plant location, and mergers and acquisitions.[12] Even before it was fully implemented, therefore, EC 92 provided European business with a stimulus—a change in regime—that required increased investment both domestic and foreign. Alexis Jacquemin and Andre Sapir note that

11. See Gasiorek, Smith, and Venables (1992). These effects are even smaller when general equilibrium effects are modeled, for example, see Haaland (1993). Three-quarters of the benefits come from greater competition, one-quarter from savings in trade costs.

12. De la Torre and Kelly (1992) quote data indicating that international merger and acquisition activity in western Europe rose sharply from $9 billion in 1986 to $52 billion in 1989.

European business restructuring has included a growing concentration on the main product lines, an extension of geographic coverage, and a multiplication of cooperative arrangements, mergers, and acquisitions.[13] Similarly, firms owned by Americans, Japanese, and residents of neighboring countries such as Switzerland and Sweden increased their stakes and rationalized their production and distribution networks to take advantage of the continental strategies that now became possible. Once firms expected competition would be Europe-wide and planned their strategies accordingly, their expectations became self-fulfilling. It is hard to believe that these effects on growth are adequately captured by even the more sophisticated general equilibrium models.

Impact on Outsiders

The EC experience sheds light on an important question that is not resolved by our theories. Has the EC in general, and the deeper integration associated with the EC and the EC 92 program in particular, led to more or less protection against outsiders? It is useful in trying to answer this question to focus on three groups: those who chose to join the EC, those who have concluded special association agreements, and members of the multilateral trading system in general.

In fact, most countries that might have been adversely affected by the formation of the Community have been able to demand and obtain compensatory "benefits." Some have avoided the trade diversion by becoming full members. Others have mitigated these effects by obtaining preferential access through free trade or association agreements. Finally, most countries of the world have been compensated either explicitly through offsetting tariff reductions or implicitly by Europe's participation in the multilateral tariff reductions. However, as I describe below, the impact of Europe's move toward deeper forms of integration has depended critically on the nature of the policies harmonized. Where deeper integration has involved coordinated sectoral policies that were inter-

13. Jacquemin and Sapir (1991, p. 166).

ventionist, outsiders have usually been hurt. By contrast, Europe's efforts at increasing the role of market forces have resulted in external benefits. In addition, however, the Union has been able to use its market power to undermine the spirit and the letter of GATT. It has insisted on numerous so-called voluntary export restraints, especially on Asian exports. Furthermore, outsiders have been vulnerable to its antidumping rules, which have often been applied in a manner that is less than transparent.

The Treaty of Rome allows other "European" nations to join the Community on condition that (a) the existing members unanimously agree and (b) the new members agree to assume the full duties of membership.[14] The formation of the European Community and its deepening relationships set in motion considerable pressures on other European nations to join the Community. Of course, access has not always been routine. France vetoed the British application in 1963, and the European Community has kept Turkey and several European Free Trade Area (EFTA) countries waiting for some time before deciding on their applications.

Even when they have not wholeheartedly endorsed the positive vision of what the Community is about, several nations have concluded that membership is essential for defensive reasons. (It is also not surprising, given their defensive motivations, that such members have been less enthusiastic about the more ambitious plans for economic and monetary union.) Despite its rejection in 1963, the United Kingdom was driven by its concerns with the potential losses from exclusion to apply for membership in 1973.[15] This move induced Ireland and Denmark to join because they, in turn, feared the diversion of their agricultural exports away from the British market.

For Greece, Spain, and Portugal, by contrast, the motives were more positive and were both economic and political. Besides seeking inclusion in the European market and the fiscal transfers Europe gives to agricultural producers and to members with poor

14. The abortive negotiations with Britain in the 1960s proved that membership conditions could not be changed.

15. See Winters (1992)

regions, all three countries entered to secure democracy and an external authority for domestic policies.

Once inside the Community, members have tried to defend against the erosion of their preferences. Greece initially opposed the entry of the Iberian nations, and today Iberia is unwilling to see liberalization in textiles and reluctant about the accession of Eastern Europe.

EFTA

The European Union is the most important trading partner of the European Free Trade Area (EFTA). Their relationship demonstrates how the movement toward deeper integration in the Union produced pressures on those most dependent on it to seek closer relations. In other words how internal deepening may lead to pressures for enlargement.[16] In the first place, EFTA was created as an alternative arrangement by seven nations, several of whom had political reservations about joining the European Economic Community.[17] However, nations that were dependent on the European Community could not afford to remain out of step as the Community's market orientation was strengthened.

Thus it was no surprise in 1972 and 1973 when EFTA nations concluded parallel bilateral free trade agreements with the European Community on most industrial goods. EFTA had been faced with the prospect of two of its members, the United Kingdom and Denmark, joining the European Community.

The EC 92 initiative offered other inducements for closer association. Although all tariffs and quantitative restrictions had been removed on trade in manufactures within the European Community and EFTA, some obstacles to free trade remained, consisting mainly of administrative procedures (border controls) and government practices (technical standards and public procurement rules). Since the program for EC 92 eliminates many of these obstacles

16. See Baldwin (1993).
17. Austria, Denmark, Norway, Portugal, Sweden, Switzerland, and the United Kingdom. Iceland joined in 1970; Finland became an associate member in 1961 and a full member in 1986.

within the Community, it places pressures on EFTA nations to do likewise. As Per Magnus Wijkman notes, after the announcement of the EC 92 program, Sweden's direct investments in the Community doubled each year in nominal dollars, raising fears that Sweden's industrial base would be transferred to the Community.[18]

In 1992, therefore, EFTA nations concluded negotiations with the Community to create a European Economic Area. The agreement established the free circulation of persons, goods, services, and capital besides the application of the same competition rules for all the signatories and the strengthening of cooperation between EFTA and the Community in fields such as research and development, the environment, consumer protection, education, social policy, and small and medium enterprises. It also created an EFTA Court of Justice and implemented Community law as a common base of reference. But the agreement on a European Economic Area did not provide EFTA countries with rights to vote on decisions shaping legislation, nor could they participate in the Common Agriculture Policy or adopt EC external tariffs. (Typically these are lower in EFTA than in the Community.)[19]

Although EFTA has entered into an arrangement that goes far deeper than a traditional free trade area (FTA), because EFTA has not harmonized its external tariffs with those of the Community, it is necessary to examine EFTA products at the Community's border to ensure they meet requirements about rules of origin.

With the end of the cold war, however, several EFTA countries, such as Austria, Switzerland, and Sweden, no longer faced the political problem of their neutrality in foreign policy as an impediment to full EC membership. In response, therefore, several EFTA countries decided that full membership in the Union would improve their relative positions, and in 1995 Sweden, Finland, and Austria joined the Union as full members. The centripetal forces of the European Union were too powerful to be resisted.

18. Wijkman (1992, p. 304).
19. For a more extensive treatment see Laredo (1992).

Preferential Access

Although the European Union is a full member of GATT, very few of its trading partners receive most favored nation treatment. Many developing countries are eligible for the EU's Generalized System of Preferences (GSP), which allows exemptions or reduced duty rates for developing countries. However, the EU has concluded an extensive network of special trading arrangements with developing and developed countries. These include agreements with EFTA, Eastern Europe, Mediterranean, African, and Caribbean nations.

Several of the countries who entered the EEC (France, Belgium, Netherlands, and Italy) had preferential arrangements with their present and former colonies. In response the Community negotiated special agreements that offered these nations preferential access for some of their exports to the Community as a whole. The Community also has agreements with Mediterranean countries, which provide preferential access but make few concessions on agricultural products to which the Community applies variable levies.

Today, Europe faces the special challenge of absorbing trade from the East. Susan Collins and Dani Rodrik estimate that eastern Europe and the former Soviet Union will eventually increase their share of world trade from 10 to 23 percent with an impact that will be especially felt by western Europe.[20] Broadening will present new adjustment problems. The export potential of eastern European countries will initially be concentrated in agricultural commodities and labor-intensive products—and thus be directly competitive with the products of the developing countries. With such broadening, a new group of insiders from eastern Europe could join nations from southern Europe who are unwilling to see their preferential position undermined by foreign competitors.

Thus far, however, Europe has not been forthcoming with market access for the east European nations. In particular, the east European nations have signed association agreements with the EU. These call for free trade by 2000 except for agriculture. The

20. Collins and Rodrik (1991).

east Europeans are given time to liberalize their markets under these treaties but are obliged to end most of the protection of their weak industries within five years.[21]

The east European nations are also expected to change their laws on matters such as competition policy to reflect EU norms, although they are not exempted from European antidumping rules.[22] The disappointing feature of the agreements is that they include restraints on so-called sensitive products such as textiles, iron, steel, coal, and chemicals. They contain provisions on export quotas, safeguards, and rules of origin that undermine their capacity to be a true cornerstone of integration between East and West.[23]

In sum, Europe has been prepared to provide concessional access to many countries. Often, since 1974, such access has not been accompanied by reciprocal concessions on European products. This has served to limit the trade-diverting impact of such agreements.

Multilateral Barriers

The formation of the EC meant raising tariffs in Germany and Benelux and lowering them in Italy and France. There is some debate in the literature over whether the Community tended to influence its more free trade members to become more protectionist or its less liberal members to become more open. Although the United States strongly supported the formation of the Community, it sought redress from the impact of the trade diversion implied by the formation of the Community. First it helped to convene the multilateral trade negotiations at GATT known as the Dillon Round, held between May 1961 and March 1962, and then the Kennedy Round held between

21. In fact, several east European nations have made marked headway toward trade liberalization. Protection in the Czech and Slovak Republics and in Poland is now lower, more uniform, and (being based largely on tariffs) more transparent than that accorded to producers in most OECD countries.

22. See Hoekman and Mavroidis (1994).

23. Although steel duties will be eliminated within five years, for example, the EC expects voluntary export restraint from Hungary.

1964 and 1967.[24] Clearly these examples show that regionalism served to reenforce multilateral liberalization.

According to Gary Hufbauer, without the prior formation of the EC, the Kennedy Round would not have taken place. He argues that "France and Italy . . . would have strongly resisted making any concessions in the 1960s, and Germany would not have made trade concessions in isolation from its continental partners"[25] By making France and Italy part of the Community, therefore, the EC played a key role in their participation in the tariff reductions in the early 1960s. Alan Winters, however, argues that the EC probably constrained Holland and Germany from being more liberal.[26]

Although Europe lowered its tariffs, this did not necessarily represent "compensation" to the rest of the world for the EC's formation, since simultaneously the EC also benefited from the reciprocal reduction of tariffs made by the United States and other GATT members. Nonetheless, this experience is not consistent with the economic theory which suggests that a larger body would become more protectionist by raising barriers to the outside world for reasons connected with the optimal tariff. It also demonstrates, as Alan Winters perceptively notes, that aggressive unilateralism can pay off.[27]

On joining the EC, Greece, Spain, and Portugal were required to lower their external barriers.[28] This experience provides some support for Jagdish Bhagwati's proposal that GATT rules for preferential trade arrangements should be confined to customs unions. Winters notes, however, that the use of nontariff barriers by the EC has increased relatively more rapidly than in other major economies. Winters cites data that suggest that coverage increased from "a relatively liberal 10 percent" in the 1950s to levels similar to those of the United States and Japan.[29]

24. During the Dillon Round, tariffs were reduced and according to Winters, Germany and Belgium went back to their original levels and average tariffs were reduced from 12.5 to 11.7 percent; during the Kennedy Round (1964–67) they were reduced even further to 8.1 percent. Scott (1992 p. 36).

25. Hufbauer (1990, p. 5).

26. Winters (1992).

27. Winters (1992).

28. As noted by de la Torre and Kelly (1992, p. 22), Spain's average tariff fell from 13 to 5 percent.

29. Winters (1992).

Sectoral Policies

The initiating step toward creating the EC was taken in the Treaty of Paris, which established the European Community of Steel and Coal and was signed in 1951. The treaty implemented a highly controlled basing-point price system that led to market-sharing arrangements among EC steelmakers. The EC policies in steel and coal have continued to be controlled and protectionist ever since. A conspicuous example was the Davignon Plan, instituted in 1977 and implemented during the 1980s, which introduced a comprehensive set of import restrictions that control both quantities and prices to bolster the market-sharing arrangements in its internal cartel.[30]

The EC has also followed EC-wide policies in textiles and apparel and shipbuilding, which have been common and protectionist. But the EC's policies in agriculture, the Common Agricultural Policy (CAP), provide the clearest demonstration that the harmonization of nonmarket-oriented policies can result in a highly protectionist regime. The CAP has generated oversupply and led to excessively high stocks and world market prices that are depressed and volatile. The CAP includes a system of domestic price supports achieved in part through variable levies on imports and subsidies for exports. By keeping prices stable and high within the Community CAP has the effect of generally depressing them and making them more volatile in the rest of the world.[31] Disputes over CAP were the central obstacle to completion of the Uruguay Round.[32]

Antidumping and Common Trade Policy

Since 1968 the Commission has been responsible for the administration of antidumping rules for all members of the EC. The

---

30. Tarr (1988).

31. See de la Torre and Kelly (1992, p. 22).

32. Hufbauer (1990, p. 31) mentions other EC-wide policies that have raised outside concerns. Protection through technical standards; denial of access to foreign firms into consortia; public procurement; subsidies (for example, Airbus); and the promotion of European champion firms. He notes, however, that some foreign-owned European-based firms have been able to participate in several consortia, some agreement has been reached on Airbus, and the issues of subsidies and public procurement were the subject of agreements at the Uruguay Round.

EC follows GATT and imposes penalties only if both injury and dumping are found. However, the application of these rules is notoriously problematic. Most cases are resolved by exporters undertaking to maintain prices above a certain level. The use of rules of origin that might qualify a product as domestic rather than imported has been extremely controversial. The United States and other major industrial countries have implemented antidumping provisions with effects similar to those of the EC. Thus it is not clear that the existence of the EC has made these policies worse than they would have been had the individual members developed their own policies independently.

There is also controversy over whether Europe as a whole has followed more protectionist voluntary export restraint policies than might have been true had its members acted independently. Winters argues that the United Kingdom and Germany would be without footwear protection today, agricultural protection in the United Kingdom would be lower, and there would be no arrangement on Japanese cars in Denmark if the EC did not exist.[33]

Deeper Integration

When the EC 92 program was being formulated, some outsiders viewed it with alarm. Indeed, many thought that Europe was becoming a fortress. This image partly reflected fears that foreign subsidiaries might not enjoy national treatment within Europe, that is, that an American-owned bank in London would not enjoy the same rights of establishment as one owned by the British. However, these fears have proved ungrounded although concerns about quotas on the sale of automobiles produced by Japanese-owned companies have proved more valid. Despite such problems, overall the market orientation of EC 92 should probably be viewed

33. Winters (1992) argues provocatively that common policies and common rules are best seen as necessary props for the common market rather than as additional objectives in their own right. He gives an interesting argument on VCRs as reflecting a desire to "communitarise" unilateral French action against Japan and also mentions French and Italian quantitative restrictions against footwear from Taiwan and Korea. Norberg (1992) provides a more ambivalent judgment on the impact of the EC on European voluntary export restraints.

as a plus for outsiders. EC 92 should provide improved access to outsiders because of the deep character of the integration it will achieve. Although it is true that a single standard can be crafted to inhibit foreign entry, a single standard can also benefit all who wish to sell in Europe, not only European firms. The average cost of meeting a single standard for all Europe is likely to be far less expensive than that of meeting twelve different standards that are required today. And if Europe successfully disciplines state aids (subsidies to industry), *all* who compete in the market will benefit. The fervor of each medium-sized European country to have a full complement of industries should wane if European nations grow accustomed to accepting the market verdict internally. If this analysis is correct, that is, that deep integration increases the access of outsiders, it implies that efforts to extend membership in the EC to EFTA and east European countries ought to enjoy support from the rest of the world.

Indeed Harry Flamm quotes the report by GATT that finds "little evidence of any recent major intensification of protective measures on the part of the EC."[34] And Jacques Pelkmans has undertaken a detailed review of the EC 92 directives and found almost no evidence that these have been implemented in a protectionist manner.[35]

Extra- and Intraregional Trade

The impact of these events on intra-European trade is evident in the data: they show the different effects of European industrial and agricultural policies.[36] Intra-EC exports as a share of all EC exports increased from less than 40 percent in 1958 to nearly 55 percent in 1970. The ratio remained roughly constant until 1985 and then increased to over 60 percent in 1990.[37]

34. Flamm (1992, pp. 26–27).
35. Pelkmans (1992).
36. De la Torre and Kelly (1992) summarize several studies on the impact of the EC. They quote studies by El-Agraa arguing that trade diversion exceeded trade creation in the first fifteen years and diversion was concentrated in agriculture.
37. Sapir (1992, p. 1492).

This recent, relative intensification of intra-European trade is mainly because of developments in agricultural trade. This reflects not EC 92 but rather the impact of the increasingly protectionist Common Agricultural Policy. Indeed, no such recent trend toward an increased share of intra-EC trade is evident in the trade data for processed and manufactured products. The EC countries have become increasingly integrated into both regional and global markets. In a sample of nine EC economies, André Sapir reports that the share of domestic products in the domestic consumption of manufactured goods declined from 66.7 percent in 1980 to 56.1 percent in 1991 with intra-EC imports increasing from 19.1 to 25 percent of consumption and extra-EC imports rising from 14.2 to 18.9 percent of consumption. By contrast, in food, drink, and tobacco there are trends toward a reduction in the share of extra-EC imports.

A longstanding trend has been the increased share of intra-EC trade that is intraindustry. As estimated by Sapir these shares rise with the levels of economic development. Europe can be divided into three groups: Greece and Portugal with 31 and 37 percent of trade taking the form of intraindustry; Denmark, Italy, Ireland, and Spain (around 60 percent), and the remaining richer nations between 75 and 83 percent.[38]

In sum, the data support the arguments that Europe's industrial trading relationships with the rest of the world have grown at the same time as its internal trade has flourished. By contrast, evidence of trade diversion is more apparent in agriculture. And as European economies have grown and become more developed, trade has increasingly involved intraindustry trade for which common rules and regulations can be important in facilitating competition.

Conclusion

The European experience suggests that economic integration is a cumulative process. Shallow integration—removing border bar-

---

38. See Sapir (1992, p. 1496). Since the mid-1970s, intra-EC investment has also increased from 25 percent of the total inward stock to 40 percent. Investment by European transnational corporations, notes Katseli (1992, p.14), accounts for more than 50 percent of the direct foreign investment in stock in France, Belgium, Italy, Portugal, and Spain.

riers and providing for national treatment—does not necessarily create genuinely integrated markets. Most likely once the gains from shallow integration are exhausted, and intraindustry trade increases, behind-the-border barriers will inevitably become the focus of attention. It remains an open question, however, whether the process must lead to full economic and monetary union.

The formation of the EC and its measures toward enlargement and deepening have produced pressures on its trading partners to conform increasingly to its standards, to reduce their barriers to EC exports, and to seek lower barriers for their products in the EC market. Instead of responding with higher tariffs as it has become larger, and as might have been expected by a naive version of the theory of optimal tariffs, Europe has also been willing to reduce its external tariff barriers, outside of agriculture. The fact that Europe has been an open arrangement has given those most adversely affected additional means to achieve mitigation by joining the EU.

The GATT rules and process, imperfect as they may have been, have been critical in providing outsiders with the means to mitigate some of the trade diversion effects. This was demonstrated clearly in the aftermath of the formation of the EEC, and it was also evident in the Uruguay Round negations.

Deep integration, that is, the achievement of harmonized regional policies, could lead to more or less protection depending on the specific nature of the policies. The EC's choice of trying to thwart market pressures in sectors such as agriculture, steel, and coal led to a Europe that was more protectionist to the outside world. And the Community's efforts to wrest control of external voluntary export restraint (VER) policies away from individual countries has probably also led to more protection for the Community as a whole. Similarly, the availability of antidumping rules has permitted producers one-stop shopping for protection that might have been more difficult to achieve in markets that were more fragmented. There is thus ample evidence of contamination.

Market-conforming measures, however, have had the opposite effect—leading to increased trade opportunities both internally and externally. European disciplines on state aids and other measures that favor domestic producers provide benefits for all who compete within Europe. Similarly, the achievement of common standards reduces costs for all who wish to sell in the market.

In sum, the move toward European unity is being driven by two competing visions. Both are based on the notion that competitiveness requires continentwide approaches, but each one has very different visions of what the policy should be. One view is that market forces should operate on a continental basis, that competition policy should be tough, and mutual recognition should introduce competition between regulatory regimes; but a second view is that intervention and rules should operate on a continental basis, that industrial policies should promote European competitors (rather than enforce competition), and Europe-wide regulatory, agricultural, and social policies should temper the effects of the market. A Europe that is more deeply integrated could in principle become more or less protectionist and closed to outsiders. A Europe that is open to new members and committed to market allocation should provide greater access to outsiders. A Europe that regulates heavily will not.

Chapter 6

North America and Beyond

*I*N THE SHORT SPACE OF A DECADE, the prospects for free trade in the Americas have changed from dim to likely. The United States has influenced this outcome by its free trade agreement with Canada in the Canada-U.S. Free Trade Agreement (CUSFTA) in 1989 and its participation in the North American Free Trade Agreement (NAFTA) with both Canada and Mexico in 1994. And throughout Central and South America bilateral and plurilateral free trade areas and customs unions have been formed or renewed. By the mid-1990s, the Western Hemisphere contained a complex array of trade linkages, with some countries participating in nine or ten such agreements. Given the extent of these arrangements and the extensive unilateral liberalization that almost every country in Central and South America has concluded, it was not surprising that in Miami in 1994 the heads of state of thirty-four countries signed an agreement to conclude talks for a free trade area of the Americas (FTAA), hemispheric in scope, by 2005 at the latest. The United States had also signed a free trade agreement with Israel, and the United States, Canada, Mexico, and Chile had joined other nations from the Asia Pacific in agreeing to free trade and investment in the APEC region by 2020.

Canada-U.S. Free Trade Agreement

As typical developed countries, neither Canada nor the United States had particularly high tariffs. Indeed, even prior to the agreement between the United States and Canada, the average tariff rate on Canadian exports to the United States was just 1 percent, and nearly 80 percent of Canadian exports entered the United States duty free. Canadian rates against dutiable U.S. products averaged 9.9 percent. Moreover, the substantial trade flows in the motor vehicles industry had already been freed under the U.S.-Canada Automotive Agreement, which was implemented in the late 1960s. Nonetheless, many Canadians argued that the removal of these remaining barriers would give Canadian firms the opportunity to realize scale economies by increasing competitive pressures within their economy.

The participants in the Canada-U.S. Free Trade Agreement had several objectives besides the removal of tariffs. Canadians sought to escape from U.S. trade rules on dumping and countervailing duties and to enjoy a safe haven from future protectionist U.S. actions.[1] America sought free access to Canada for direct foreign investment, entry into several Canadian service sectors in which U.S. firms were particularly competitive, and the curtailment of Canadian industrial policies and subsidies.

The agreement certainly did not reflect the desire of either country to eventually move toward a political union. Nor, for that matter, did these countries seek to form a common market with a single external trade policy and the full mobility of labor. Nonetheless, despite its limited goals, the agreement provides a vivid example of the sometimes tortuous trade-offs that the partners made between achieving their goals and simultaneously retaining their sovereignty. It is apparent that these compromises prevented the full attainment of the goals sought by the agreement's proponents.

Although the agreement made some progress in moving beyond GATT, except for a few areas, it contains few examples of agreement on a common set of rules. Indeed, in several respects the agreement barely met the standards for a free trade area as outlined in Article 24 of GATT.

The agreement eliminated tariffs and nontariff barriers but contained some noteworthy sectoral exceptions. It promised that

---

1. According to Cox and Harris (1986) Canada would be better off with preferential access to a free trade area with a protected United States than it would be under multilateral free trade.

most favored nation treatment would apply to *new* service provisions, although at the same time it exempted many important sectors from even these future arrangements. It achieved some preferential access for U.S. investors by raising the transaction limit for screening provisions of Investment Canada, but it did not achieve complete investment freedom for U.S. investors. Nor did Canadians achieve exemption from U.S. trade rules: the agreement did improve their ability to challenge such rulings through representation on a binational dispute settlement body, but the issue to be judged was simply whether U.S. (or Canadian) laws had been carried out appropriately. The countries did not harmonize or eliminate these rules.

Half Full?

Richard G. Lipsey and Murray G. Smith, enthusiastic supporters of the agreement, argued that the agreement allowed Canada to achieve considerably more than it could have by simply adhering to GATT at the time.[2] Among the achievements they mention are the following:

—Increased access to the U.S. market—more tariff reductions, including the elimination of tariffs on products such as textiles, clothing, petrochemicals, and steel and the prohibition of a number of quantitative restrictions.

—Preferential treatment in U.S. contingency protection.

The use of the escape clause (Article 201 of the U.S. Trade Act) against Canadian products is restricted, and unless Canada is explicitly mentioned in legislation, it is exempt from any U.S. trade-restricting law. When Canada is mentioned in legislation, it must first be consulted.

—Mutual recognition of test data and efforts to promote harmonization of standards.

—The inclusion of most commercial services.

—Changes in dispute settlement. Instead of the traditional process by which countervailing duties and antidumping decisions are subject to internal judicial review, such decisions were made sub-

2. Lipsey and Smith (1989).

ject to binding review by a binational panel. Changes to trade laws were subject to review to determine their consistency with the agreement and with GATT.

—Finally, Lipsey notes that Canadian concessions on investment, though mild by world standards, caused a political uproar in Canada.

Half Empty?

As its free trade critics point out, however, in important respects, the Canada-U.S. agreement did not fully live up to the GATT requirement of removing "substantially all barriers" to trade in goods. As Leonard Waverman has noted, in the agreement certain goods were only partially covered—in particular agriculture; trade in some goods remained constrained—textiles; and certain goods were excluded from the agreement, for example, beer.[3]

The agreement also took only a first step toward genuine liberalization in services. Several important sectors were excluded (basic telecommunications, transportation, culture, media, doctors, dentists, lawyers, and child care), while liberalization was constrained in other sectors since existing discrimination was grandfathered. Nor did the agreement achieve complete freedom for foreign investment. Investment remained restricted in financial services, transportation, Crown corporations, and investment related to government procurement. Although the threshold size of U.S. investments that had to be reviewed by Investment Canada was raised, large investments remained subject to such review. Each country retained the sovereign right to implement its own contingent protection, although a binational panel was established as the final arbiter in trade disputes. The agreement also made little new progress in designing procedures to deal with differences in standards. Nor was any progress made on the issue of subsidies.

In sum, therefore, although the agreement did move beyond GATT in several respects, its achievements in liberalizing ser-

3. Waverman (1991).

vices and dealing with behind-the-border barriers remained fairly modest.

External Effects

Compared with the rest of the world, Canada and the United States have relatively low rates of protection for manufactured goods, and much of their bilateral trade before their FTA was not subject to any tariffs at all, which suggests the agreement gave rise to fairly limited trade diversion. Nonetheless, discrimination did occur in textiles and clothing, chemicals, lumber, steel, tires, and agriculture.[4] Discrimination could also result from rules-of-origin and government procurement practices.

Given the relatively minor accomplishments of the agreement, it is perhaps no surprise that after the conclusion of the agreement, Canadians felt considerable frustration because it did not eliminate their concerns about the operation of U.S. trade laws. To do so additional integrative measures would have had to be taken, for example, the substitution of the joint administration of competition policies for the antidumping rules and a more extensive agreement on subsidies to allow for the removal of countervailing duties. The administration of rules of origin has also been a highly controversial source of friction.

More surprising was the controversy that the agreement engendered in Canada. It polarized Canadians over the issues of the optimal role for government in their society and their relationship to the United States. The agreement was followed by macroeconomic conditions, a recession, and an appreciation of the Canadian dollar whose effects were ascribed by many to the Canada-U.S. agreement.

Nonetheless, the agreement stimulated both regional and multilateral liberalization. The Canada-U.S. Free Trade Agreement was the first of the major recent free trade agreements in the Americas. It laid the foundation for the trilateral NAFTA. It also demonstrated the willingness of the United States to follow a multitrack

4. De la Torre and Kelly (1992, p. 21).

approach to liberalization and thereby motivated other nations to make the multilateral system more effective.

NAFTA

The North American Free Trade Agreement must be understood in the context of the broader reforms implemented by the Mexican government, starting in the mid-1980s. Unlike some nations entering free trade negotiations, Mexico did not seek to perpetuate its traditional policies. Indeed, Mexico was reducing external restrictions along with its internal liberalization and privatization. Adopting new, U.S.-type institutional practices in several areas, therefore, seemed natural. Mexico did not seek an FTA with Canada and the United States to avoid liberalization with the rest of the world. On the contrary, NAFTA complemented an outwardly oriented policy, which was based on attracting foreign investment.

Credibility of Mexico's Reforms

Much of the appeal of NAFTA was that it gave credibility, permanence, and prominence to Mexico's liberalization measures. Given Mexico's long history of government intervention and troubled history with foreign investors, some foreigners (and Mexicans) were skeptical about Mexico's liberalization efforts while others were ignorant about the changed opportunities Mexico provided. NAFTA helped convince outsiders that these changes were real. Mexican leaders who followed President Carlos de Gortari Salinas would pay a considerable price in the form of damaged relations with the United States if they tried to renege on NAFTA.

Mexico also wanted secure access to its major trading partner to persuade investors to use it as an export platform, another rationale for NAFTA. Like Canada, Mexico sought to shield itself from the application of U.S. trade rules and protectionist actions. Mexico would also gain a competitive advantage over other low-wage countries because of the superior access to U.S. and Canadian markets it could provide.

Arvind Panagaryia voices skepticism about the value of these benefits to Mexico.[5] He argues that Mexico could as easily achieve credibility by locking in liberalization through GATT as through NAFTA. However, he overlooks several points. First, as I will demonstrate, the coverage of NAFTA is more extensive and comprehensive than that of the Uruguay Round. Importantly, NAFTA allowed for reforms related to foreign investment to be locked in. Second, for developing countries, GATT tariff bindings are not especially credible because before the Uruguay Round agreement, the dispute settlement procedure in GATT was very weak. In any case, Article 18 of GATT gives developing countries the right to renegotiate to raise tariffs to protect infant industries. Third, to American investors a commitment to the U.S. government (which could be enforced bilaterally) differs from a similar commitment to a multilateral body such as GATT over which the U.S. government has much less influence. Fourth, Mexican exporters and investors receive preferential treatment in the U.S. market. That makes them more likely to resist backsliding than GATT commitments, which are less extensive and provided unconditionally. Finally, even after Mexico joined GATT, President Salinas felt frustrated at the lack of interest by investors. Panagaryia claims that Mexico's reforms were sufficiently credible before NAFTA's implementation to attract foreign investment. However, direct foreign investment inflows into Mexico, which averaged $2.5 billion between 1988 and 1990, increased dramatically to an average $4.7 billion once negotiations for NAFTA began.[6]

Provisions

NAFTA was a unique achievement because it implements virtually complete free trade between two highly developed economies and a developing country within fifteen years.[7] Remarkably for

5. Panagariya (1994).
6. Cooperation (1995, p. 69).
7. Mexico and the United States will have complete free trade within fifteen years, as will Canada and Mexico except for poultry, dairy, and eggs.

trade between countries at very different development levels, NAFTA will remove all border barriers to trade, including those in previously highly protected trade in agriculture and in textiles and automobiles that meet North American content requirements.[8] The agreement is also remarkable in allowing no special and differential treatment for Mexico as a developing country.[9]

NAFTA also aims at liberalizing foreign investment and trade in services.[10] NAFTA covers all services with obligations for national treatment and rights of establishment unless the service is explicitly excluded. Significantly, the service chapter of NAFTA follows a negative list approach—listing the sectors not covered by the agreement rather than those that are. This approach implies that free trade will exist in all new service areas. Moreover, by forcing countries to list the sectors in which restrictions remain, a focus for further negotiations becomes apparent. By contrast, with the positive list approach (applied in the Canada-U.S. agreement and the General Agreement on Trade in Services [GATS] in the Uruguay Round) sectors with barriers remain hidden, and new sectors are protected unless they are explicitly recognized.

NAFTA institutes a binational appeals mechanism that can replace existing judicial review by national administrative agencies. It provides a review mechanism to monitor changes in antidumping and countervailing duty laws as applied to partner countries. NAFTA also includes a fairly substantial package on government procurement that goes further than the Canada-U.S. agreement by covering both services and construction.[11]

NAFTA allows for accession by other nations provided that current members approve. The agreement also defines rules of origin to establish which products are eligible for preferential

8. Mexico will eliminate its quotas and trade balance requirements on car imports, for example.

9. Mexico will phase out its border processing zones—the *maquiladoras* program.

10. Mexico will lift foreign investment restrictions on fourteen of nineteen basic petrochemicals, and Pemex will open its procurement to U.S. and Canadian participation within ten years. Mexico will also allow foreign investment in sectors, such as financial services, which have previously excluded it.

11. It includes procurement by agencies such as the U.S. Army Corps of Engineers, the Canadian Departments of Transportation and Fisheries, and Mexico's Pemex and Electricity Departments.

treatment. In general the rules require that goods must have been subject to sufficient transformation within North America to have had their tariff heading changed. However, a number of sector-specific rules are also applied.

On the initiative of the Clinton administration, three accords were signed to go along with NAFTA. They cover the environment, labor issues, and import surges. These accords establish new institutions to monitor conditions, to promote compliance, and to administer new dispute settlement procedures. These side agreements allowed for fines to be levied and trade sanctions (suspension of NAFTA benefits) to be applied.

Deeper Integration?

NAFTA is a striking contrast with the Canada-U.S. agreement in several respects. NAFTA's sectoral coverage is more comprehensive and contains more concessions on national sovereignty. The service liberalization under the Canada-U.S. agreement listed only the sectors that the agreement would cover. The Canada-U.S. agreement did not include provisions for most favored nation treatment in sectors not covered by the agreement. This meant that in those sectors Canadians (Americans) could be treated worse than other foreigners. By contrast, most favored nation treatment is conferred under NAFTA. The rules of origin adopted in NAFTA are generally more restrictive than those in the Canada-U.S. agreement, especially for textiles, some electronics products, and automobiles.[12]

In most respects NAFTA members are free to follow domestic policies, but in several areas, such as the administration of trade rules, labor, and environmental policies, the enforcement of each

12. In the Canada-U.S. agreement, textiles satisfied the origin rule if the fabrics with which they were produced originated in the region. Under NAFTA, however, both yarns and fabrics must originate in the region. Color televisions under the Canada-U.S. agreement were required to have 50 percent value-added. Under NAFTA, for TVs above fourteen inches, the color picture tube or the funnel or front panel of the picture tube must originate in North America. After 1999 the requirements are even more extensive. NAFTA also changed the method of evaluating the origin of automotive parts and will require 62.5 percent local content versus 50 under the Canada-U.S. agreement. Japan (1995, p. 313).

nation's own laws is subject to international scrutiny and the threat of trade sanctions. Although a common set of rules and institutional harmonization has not been attempted, therefore, efforts have been made, within the treaty and in parallel to it, to ensure the protection of intellectual property and mitigate environmental problems linked with trade and to do so by not relying entirely on voluntary national compliance. Nonetheless, countries remain free to avoid such sanctions by changing rules that they are found not to enforce. Thus the new side agreements still represent relatively small constraints on sovereignty.

The agreement covering disputes between investors and governments allows complainants to initiate proceedings through the International Convention for Settlement of Investment Disputes or the United Nations Commission on International Law (UNCITRAL) once all other measures are exhausted.[13] Thus Mexico is repudiating the Calvo doctrine under which countries do not allow foreigners to intervene in disputes over foreign investment.

NAFTA moved considerably beyond the Uruguay Round agreement in liberalizing trade in foreign investment, services, and intellectual property rights.[14] In NAFTA investment rules, the restrictions on performance requirements are more extensive than those in the Uruguay Round. The agreement on intellectual property includes products that were under development when the agreement was signed—these were excluded from the Uruguay Round coverage. The agreement on services lists services not subject to the agreement (a negative list approach) and extends national treatment coverage to all other sectors, whereas the General Agreement on Trade in Services (GATS) applies only to sectors that are listed. The definition of an investment under NAFTA is broader than that under trade-related investment measures (TRIMs). TRIMs relate only to goods, and GATS covers only

13. See Gestrin and Rugman (1995) from whom this discussion on investment provisions is drawn.

14. As noted by Sauvé (1994), there are numerous weaknesses in GATS. The core provisions of market access and national treatment are not general obligations but apply selectively to scheduled sectors and modes of supply. Perversely, many countries limit benefits to those establishing a foreign presence.

operating service establishments because portfolio investors and commercial real estate are included.

Unresolved

NAFTA can thus be classified as a genuine GATT-plus agreement. However, in numerous areas it goes no further than GATT. NAFTA does not make progress in harmonizing competition policies or eliminating administered protection in antidumping and subsidies.[15] Furthermore, no specific agreements were signed on subsidies. In these respects, NAFTA remains a much "shallower" arrangement than the European Union or the Closer Economic Relations Agreement between Australia and New Zealand in which competition policies replaced administered protection.

The NAFTA Debate

Both NAFTA itself and the debate over its ratification demonstrate the problems and benefits from minilateral agreements that go beyond GATT and in particular, the problems these arrangements pose for countries with different development levels.

Notably, although the Canada-U.S. agreement sparked a heated debate in Canada, it was barely noticed in the United States. The United States has almost three times as much trade with Canada as with Mexico, yet the similarities between Canadian and U.S. institutions made the prospect of free trade with Canada a fairly routine issue for the general U.S. electorate. In Canada, however, there were more concerns about system differences, namely, that the United States represented a threat to the Canadian welfare system.

In the United States, the Canada-U.S. agreement was seen as involving trade experts and interested industries and cities. The NAFTA discussion in the United States was much more politically salient, and the debate was highly charged. Its opponents argued that NAFTA meant a fundamental threat to U.S. domestic institu-

15. The obligations on domestic support and export subsidies are merely hortatory. NAFTA gives up on the effort to abandon subsidy and countervailing duty rules, which was mandated in the Canada-U.S. free trade agreement.

tions, especially ones affecting the environment and labor standards. Some concerns related to the direct impact of economic development in Mexico on the Mexican environment in general, especially its northern border area. But others feared that Mexico would offer a safe haven to U.S. firms who wished to evade U.S. regulations on worker safety and environment, thereby leading to a "leveling down" pressure in the United States.

The idea that trade should not occur between countries whose institutions and internal regulatory regimes are "too different" does not fit with the theory of comparative advantage as reflected in traditional trade theory. Nonetheless, it would probably have been impossible to obtain a NAFTA agreement between Canada, the United States, and Mexico, without addressing some of the concerns about the differences in regulatory arrangements. Implicitly, therefore, the NAFTA experience suggests that free trade and investment between partners with very different regulatory regimes may not be achievable without some institutional adaptation. Nonetheless the NAFTA side agreements did not harmonize labor or environmental rules. Instead they concentrated on the issue of compliance. And notably, the election of the Republican majority in the U.S. Congress in 1994 shifted power toward U.S. policymakers who believe that free trade agreements should not include provisions for labor standards and the environment. Indeed a difference of opinion over this issue became a source of controversy when the administration sought so-called fast track authority to negotiate Chile's accession to NAFTA.

NAFTA opponents in the United States also argued that NAFTA would have major consequences for U.S. employment.[16] Ross Perot made the memorable prediction that NAFTA would give rise to "a giant sucking sound" as jobs left the United States for Mexico. In fact, much of the popular debate over NAFTA focused on its employment impact rather than its effects on welfare. The consensus of most studies was that for the United States these effects would be fairly minor when compared with the size of the U.S. labor market.[17]

16. See Perot and Choate (1993).
17. See Lustig, Bosworth, and Lawrence (1992); Hufbauer and Schott (1992).

However, NAFTA has also been assailed by Multilateral/Free traders. Panagyria argues that NAFTA would reduce Mexican welfare since its exports were already granted access to the United States and Canada at very low tariff rates, while Mexican protection remained sufficiently high to induce substantial trade diversion.[18] Most empirical studies, however, especially those taking account of scale economies and increased investment showed gains for Mexico on the order of 5 percent of GNP.[19] John Whalley argues that the effects of NAFTA are likely to be smaller than those simulated in many studies because they generally assume full free trade will be achieved, whereas the agreement's complex provisions contain lots of loopholes.[20]

Free trade skeptics are concerned about NAFTA's complex rules of origin. These rules are seen as problems because they are likely to increase trade diversion; they are likely to make further accession into the agreement more difficult since they are designed with certain trading partners in mind, and they are likely to lead to extensive and expensive customs procedures.[21]

Concerns about NAFTA's impacts on outsiders are also prevalent.[22] Primo Braga summarizes the findings of studies on that subject. They suggest that effects would not be large. Typically, U.S. imports from the rest of the world would decline by less than 1 percent with very minor changes occurring in the terms of trade.[23] Even these small changes are mitigated if it is assumed that NAFTA has dynamic effects that stimulate growth and thus raise imports from the rest of the world. The impact is somewhat more significant in some sectors such as sugar and textiles, and for some countries, such as those from the Caribbean, whose preferences NAFTA eroded.

18. Panagariya (1994).

19. For a review see the chapter by Brown in Lustig, Bosworth, and Lawrence (1992, pp. 26–68).

20. Whalley (1993).

21. See Krueger (1993a); Vernon (1994).

22. Panagariya (1994).

23. For example, Primo Braga (1992, p. 217) quotes a study by Samuel Laird suggesting a decrease of only 0.72 percent in the value of exports from other countries in the Western Hemisphere to the United States. For industrialized countries a NAFTA limited to tariff elimination would mean a decrease of only 0.55 percent of exports to the United States.

Outsiders will also benefit if NAFTA succeeds in reinforcing the internal liberalization of the Mexican economy. Once Mexico makes promises to the United States to permit foreign investment, enforce intellectual property rights, and unwind its elaborate protectionist programs for automobiles and electronics, all its trading partners, not just the United States, will benefit.[24] Economic theory suggests that a free trade agreement will be welfare enhancing as long as outsiders are compensated through lower tariffs for any diversion of trade. Given Mexico's prior liberalization, outsiders were compensated in advance.

The Peso Crisis

In December 1994 Mexico's economy experienced a major currency crisis. With the benefit of hindsight it is clear that Mexico chose for too long to maintain an overvalued exchange rate to help reduce inflation. Some have interpreted the crisis as demonstrating that NAFTA was a failure. On the contrary, the crisis showed that Mexico had succeeded in its key goal of increasing its capacity to borrow. Unfortunately, however, it made poor use of its improved ability to borrow, financing capital flight when it should have made earlier adjustments. Nonetheless, the United States responded strongly to the crisis and greatly helped in providing Mexico with liquidity. The crisis demonstrated that NAFTA had contributed to closer economic relations between the United States and Mexico. Notably, Mexico did not respond to the crisis by increasing trade protection.

Nonetheless the crisis underscored the fact that modelers, by considering only the trade effects of NAFTA and its impact on long-term capital formation, erred in downplaying the macroeconomic impact of an agreement focused on investment at least as much as on trade.[25]

24. The intellectual property agreement in the Uruguay Round requires most favored nation treatment. Thus nations from outside NAFTA will receive increased intellectual property protection because NAFTA's obligations are more extensive.

25. In comments written in 1992 I emphasized that by ignoring the exchange rate, conventional models underestimated the adjustment problems posed by NAFTA for Mexico and overestimated them for the United States. I also stressed the likelihood that the peso would strengthen in the short run but weaken over the long run. See Lustig, Bosworth, and Lawrence (1992, pp. 65–66).

Accession and Next Steps

NAFTA's accession clause is vague and offers little guidance as to whether it will be a building block for a more elaborate free trade arrangement. The clause states that "any country or group of countries" may join as long as they negotiate terms that are then ratified by each NAFTA country. Conspicuously absent is a clear-cut docking clause that would guarantee access to nations who met certain conditions. The clause also does not stipulate the geographic location of new members. Clearly, however, individually or as a group, NAFTA countries will not confine their liberalization to one another.

NAFTA is not a customs union. None of the partners is willing to give up its autonomy in trade policy. The United States especially is a global trader. Canada accounts for about one-fifth of U.S. trade and Mexico around 7 percent, so the United States cannot afford to neglect trade relations outside NAFTA. The United States therefore felt compelled to accompany moves toward free trade in North America with similar policies toward other trading partners in the region and beyond.

At roughly the same time as he announced his intention to negotiate a free trade agreement with Mexico, President Bush announced an Enterprise for the Americas initiative, which called for lowering debt, raising investment, and a series of free trade agreements with the nations of Latin America, either separately or in groups. At the same time as he agreed to negotiations to extend NAFTA to Chile at the Summit of the Americas, which took place in Miami in December 1994, President Clinton helped launch the agreement by thirty-four nations in the Americas to conclude negotiations on a free trade area for the Americas by 2005. Just one month earlier, the NAFTA countries had announced their participation in the Bogor commitment for free trade in the Asia-Pacific Economic (APEC) region by 2020.

Mexico also moved to complement its membership in NAFTA by negotiating free trade agreements with numerous nations to its south. Mexico concluded such agreements with Chile, Caricom, Colombia, Venezuela, Costa Rica, and Bolivia. It also joined APEC and the Organization for Economic Cooperation and Development.

The Enterprise for the Americas initiative launched by the Bush administration was enthusiastically received throughout Latin America, demonstrating the powerful pressures for inclusion that NAFTA had generated. In NAFTA Mexico gains a competitive benefit over Latin American nations located nearby. Naturally, those nations seek to offset Mexico's advantage.

Many countries throughout Latin America, therefore, are eager to join NAFTA or an alternative arrangement to achieve free trade in the Americas. Washington has signed numerous framework agreements with many countries separately and with the Mercosur customs union as a group (Argentina, Brazil, Paraguay, and Uruguay). These agreements are viewed as precursors to full free trade agreements.

Of course, Canada and Mexico might be reluctant to see their preferences eroded by extensions of NAFTA. But the United States could simply bypass them and sign separate agreements with other nations. Given that their preferences would be eroded in any case, they clearly have an interest in being included in additional agreements, which also makes sense for the United States administratively. Thus it is no surprise that Canada participated in NAFTA negotiations and that both partners would like to negotiate with Chile. Such participation bodes well for the future. It increases the likelihood of a single more inclusive arrangement to cover the Americas as a whole rather than a crazy-quilt system with a multiplicity of rules.[26]

In sum, NAFTA is an agreement whose scope exceeds that of GATT. Its accomplishment in bringing about free trade between a developing and two highly developed economies is considerable. It has also set in motion a process that is expanding with a strong gravitational force. Skeptics suggest that Latin American countries who join NAFTA will experience more trade diversion than trade creation. But the fact that these nations can in turn sign agree-

26. Kowalczyk and Wonnacott (1992) show that countries that form the spokes in a hub-and-spoke arrangement have lower welfare than those that participate in a conventional free trade agreement. However, the country forming the hub, by having preferred access to the spokes may do better than a free trade agreement (although this is not always true). Spokes will thus generally be inclined to prefer a free trade agreement to a hub-and-spoke arrangement.

ments with other nations in Europe, Asia, and elsewhere will allow them to offset these effects and to retain the benefits of deeper liberalization than the GATT/World Trade Organization system has thus far been able to deliver. However, the most important unfinished business in NAFTA is achieving agreements on competition policies and subsidies, which would allow elimination of administered protection through antidumping and countervailing duty provisions. And the most important deficiency in NAFTA is its rules of origin, especially for products such as textiles, automobiles, and televisions, which clearly discriminate against outsiders and inevitably inhibit the flow of all trade across North American borders.

Chapter 7

Asia and the Pacific

*T*HE EAST ASIAN NATIONS did not participate in the first phase of global regionalism among developing countries in the 1960s.[1] Although seven nations in the area did form the Association of Southeast Asian nations (ASEAN), it remained essentially a political association with a few, relatively small programs designed to promote intra-ASEAN trade, joint ventures, and industrial specialization. More recently, however, ASEAN joined the global trend toward free trade areas, when, in 1992, these nations agreed to implement an ASEAN free trade area (AFTA) by 2007.[2] The major regional initiative in the Pacific is the Asia-Pacific Economic Cooperation (APEC) forum, an association that includes nations from Asia, Australasia, and North and South America. APEC seeks to promote the development and growth of its members through increased trade and investment, but to do so in a way that also strengthens and supports the multilateral trading system.

To appreciate the driving forces behind APEC, it is useful to review several key features of the region. The first is the market-led process of economic integration that has already taken place in Asia; the second is the great stake that many of the nations in the region place in the multilateral trading system; and the third are

1. Defined as Japan, the Asian newly industrializing economies (Korea, Taiwan, Singapore, and Hong Kong) and the Association of Southeast Asian nations (ASEAN) (Brunei, Indonesia, Malaysia, Philippines, Singapore, and Thailand).

2. Although all are outwardly oriented, with the exception of Singapore, ASEAN countries, for example, actually have small shares of their trade with one another.

79

the weak incentives that exist for concluding large, formal free trade agreements in East Asia alone. Each of these forces has helped give APEC its unique character: its broad range of membership—including nations from both sides of the Pacific, its emphasis on open regionalism and trade facilitation as well as liberalization, and the reluctance on the part of some of its members to engage in a traditional process of free trade liberalization.

Market-Led Integration

The lack of formal initiatives to encourage regional integration has not prevented it from taking place in Asia. As measured by trade and investment flows, integration within the Asian region has accelerated since the mid-1980s. The share of intraregional trade in overall East Asian trade has increased rapidly. There is some debate about whether this integration reflects a bias of these nations to trade with one another or whether it results simply from the more conventional determinants of trade and integration, but most of the evidence points to the latter.[3] As Frankel has emphasized, the intra-Asian trade share is growing because Asia is growing rapidly, and fast-growing economies tend to have increasing shares of trade with one another.

Asian economies are diverse in per capita income, size, openness, and natural resource endowments. This diversity leads to considerable room for specialization. Before the mid-1980s, Japan specialized in human capital and technology-intensive products; economies such as Hong Kong, Korea, Singapore, and Taiwan in unskilled labor-intensive products, and other Asian countries such as Malaysia, Philippines, and Thailand and Indonesia in products that are natural resource intensive. These patterns have shifted, however, because of the transfer of technology and foreign investment. Over the 1980s, as Kiichiro Fukasaku shows, economies such as Korea, Taiwan, and Singapore shifted from unskilled labor toward technology and products that are human capital intensive,

3. For reviews of the evidence see Lincoln (1992); Saxonhouse (1993); Frankel (1993); Lawrence (1991); and Urata (1993).

and others with lower wage levels moved away from reliance on products that are natural resource intensive into producing labor-intensive manufactured goods.[4]

It would also be erroneous to infer that the intensification of regional trading relations among Asian nations represents a shift toward greater self-sufficiency. Indeed, the need to compete more effectively in global markets has intensified regional specialization patterns. Regional and global trade seem to be complements rather than substitutes, with firms investing in Asia and integrating their production regionally with a view to servicing regional and global markets. The regionalization of Asian trade and growth reflects the beneficial spillover effects occurring when a group of countries simultaneously adopts outward-oriented policies. Countries following export-oriented strategies create markets for their trading partners. If value-added domestically is to compete in the world market it has to meet global standards of quality and price. An essential feature of such strategies, therefore, is providing access to key inputs (technology, capital, and intermediate inputs) at world prices. Thus successful exporters provide growing markets for suppliers of these inputs from other countries—many of whom are neighbors.

The production process in Asia has become increasingly internationalized. Key capital goods come from Japan; labor-intensive assembly operations are performed in low-wage countries such as China, Indonesia, Thailand, and even Vietnam; and Hong Kong, Singapore, and Taiwan provide more sophisticated operations such as design, marketing, and finance. Despite some reputation for exclusion and protection, therefore, Asia has been capable of generating a rapid increase in trade owing to growth and a virtuous regional circle with thick networks forming.

Subregional economic zones exemplify this complementarity. Several neighboring provinces of different countries have become closely linked through trade and investment.[5] It is also striking,

4. See Fukasaku (1992). See also Yokota and Imaoka (1993), who find that the trade structures of Korea, Hong Kong, Singapore, and Taiwan have become similar to that of Japan, and those of the ASEAN countries have become similar to these four.

5. See Chia and Lee (1993). These include the growth triangle centered on Singapore and including Johor state of Malaysia and Batam Island of Indonesia; the Baht zone in the border area of Thailand, Laos, and Cambodia; the Greater South China economic zone

and typical of Asian developments, that these zones have sometimes flourished despite rather than because of explicit government policies. As Peter Drysdale and Ross Garnaut observe, the
most rapidly expanding intra-East Asian bilateral trading relationships, China and Taiwan and China and Korea, have developed around and despite discriminatory restrictions on bilateral
trade.[6]

Support for GATT

The literature is filled with debates about the reasons for Asia's
success. Although many Asian countries have shared in that success, they have done so while following policies that were very
different in their degree of domestic intervention and protection.
Some countries, like Hong Kong and Singapore, have been open;
others like Japan and Korea initially developed behind high barriers. However, all the successful nations have placed the highest
priority on stimulating exports of manufactured goods.

Consequently, despite their diversity, Asian nations are united
in their support for the multilateral trading system that emerged
under GATT. For these nations GATT contains several very attractive features. First, GATT has been successful in lowering the
border barriers that previously inhibited the access of Asian products to developed country markets. More recently GATT has
taken steps to liberalize agricultural trade.

Second, GATT provides for special and preferential treatment
for developing countries—a category into which most Asian countries fall. Consequently these countries enjoy considerable scope
for domestic policy autonomy. Under the permissive environment
provided by GATT, import barriers in developing countries can be
high or low. Similarly, foreign investment can be promoted or
prohibited. GATT also allowed developed economies such as

---

centered on Hong Kong and including Guandong, Macao, and Fujian in China and
Taiwan. It also includes the Yellow Sea zone (China, Korea, Japan) and the Japan Sea
(China, Russia, North and South Korea, and Japan).

6. See Drysdale and Garnaut (1993).

Japan a large scope for domestic policy autonomy. This freedom was important for nations with unusual institutions since it preserved their right to be different.

Third, GATT outlawed managed trade, especially the use of quota protection—precisely the form of protection that had been directed against rapidly growing new exporters. Since GATT emphasized rules-based solutions countries acquired protection against demands for results through managed trade. Admittedly GATT was not wholly successful in enforcing this rule, but to be so, a tougher rather than weaker GATT would be required.

Fourth, as a multilateral institution, GATT offered smaller countries protection from the political pressures of more powerful trading partners. Keeping trade depoliticized is an important goal in Asia where political tensions run high and there are large imbalances of power. The GATT system offered the only realistic means for restraining the United States in its bilateral initiatives and its demands for export shares.

Skepticism about Regionalism

At the same time as they have strongly supported the GATT approach, many Asians have been skeptical of regionalism both as it is now emerging outside of the region and as an approach to promoting trade within the region. Several Asian countries have watched developments of EC 1992 and NAFTA with great suspicion. Europe may not have become a protectionist "fortress" as some feared, but with its use of voluntary export restraints, and its insistence on reciprocity, it appears to many Asians to have a rampart facing east.

Furthermore, for at least four reasons, Asians face great obstacles to forming arrangements of their own that are patterned after those in Europe and North America.

Successful Performance

First, Asia's economic performance has been successful. Regional growth and integration in Asia have thrived with little international governmental oversight. By contrast, the drive for regional integration programs elsewhere was partly motivated by the need to change the direction of policy. EC 92, for example, was a response to slow European growth in the early 1980s. Similarly, Canada and Mexico turned to the United States when their performance was in trouble and Latin American economies liberalized in part through regional agreements in the face of the debt crisis. Although Asians have adjusted to success by liberalization, they have not sought to radically change their economic institutions in the same way as those who have been less successful have changed. They are less willing to import foreign institutions and arrangements that might be associated with a formal regional arrangement.

Political

The second reason is political. Unlike Europeans few Asians nurture the dream of eventually becoming a United States of Asia. Many neighboring nations are still affected by their history of enmity and competition. The distribution of power in Asia is uneven. This makes smaller nations unwilling to risk regionwide agreements that might be dominated by large players such as Japan and/or China and reluctant to conclude arrangements that exclude these economies for fear of their response.

Japanese efforts at achieving economic hegemony in the region in the 1930s have cast a long shadow, leading to reluctance by both Japan and other nations to conclude arrangements that evoke historical memories. Although suspicions are weakening, they remain significant. Given its economic prominence, Japan would inevitably have to assume a leadership role in a purely Asian regional arrangement. Neither China nor Korea would welcome an arrangement dominated by Japan.

Political problems associated with China remain a significant obstacle for its inclusion in any formal arrangement, while an arrangement excluding China would not be welcomed by a country dramatically increasing its external economic relations. Finally, the United States retains military, political, and economic power in the region and would not take kindly to an arrangement from which it was excluded.

Few Sticks

Several nations outside Asia have sought membership in regional arrangements to provide safe havens for their trading relationships. When the six European nations formed the EEC, or EC, they set up a gravitational force that attracted their neighbors. The deeper these relationships, the stronger the costs of exclusion appeared to become. This stick of exclusion has acted as a major stimulus, prompting nations to seek membership in the EC. Similarly, Canada and Mexico are highly dependent on the U.S. market and were induced to seek free trade agreements partly to obtain shelter from U.S. protectionism. Other nations in Latin America have been attracted to NAFTA, partly to restore their relative position in comparison with Mexico.

Developing Asian economies do not depend on the Japanese market to the degree that Mexico and Canada depend on the United States. Nor has the Japanese market become more protectionist in recent years—indeed it has become more open. Accordingly, although Asian nations might welcome the carrot of increased access to the Japanese market, they do not fear the stick of increased Japanese protection. The only major "stick" that might induce an Asian arrangement would be a breakdown in the global trading system. If indeed, for example, the EU and America formed protectionist blocks, Asia might feel compelled to respond. However, although many in Asia harbor fears about foreign protectionist blocks, they have not formed.

Policy Changes

Finally, moving to a regional arrangement would require great adjustment and policy changes in many countries. Although most countries in Asia are members of GATT, as developing countries many have not yet fully accepted the obligations of GATT. For economies such as Hong Kong and Singapore, a formal free trade agreement would afford few adjustment costs. However, protection remains significant in many Asia countries. Although tariffs have been declining in East Asia, in most countries they remain fairly high.[7] As Soogil Young has argued, therefore, given the high current levels of protection, an East Asian free trade block could result in considerable trade diversion.[8] Moreover, several Asian economies pursue interventionist industrial policies. Countries are unwilling to give up policies that they believe have been successful. The use of infant industry protection for nurturing new industries would surely be problematic in a free trade regime.

APEC: Four Adjectives in Search of a Noun?[9]

These considerations have been important in shaping the major initiative for regional arrangements in the Asia-Pacific known as APEC (Asia-Pacific Economic Cooperation). They explain why APEC had fairly humble beginnings and was initially greeted with skepticism. APEC was originally proposed in early 1989 by Australian Prime Minister Bob Hawke. It started with meetings between foreign and economic ministers and with several relatively small projects. APEC has grown in scope and prominence, however, and achieved a more significant status with the agreement to hold annual summit meetings of heads of state. The first took place in 1993 on Blake Island in Seattle, and the second occurred in 1994 in Bogor, Indonesia.

The diversity of APEC's membership is notable. APEC is an inclusive arrangement with nations from both sides of the Pacific. This diversity reflects the needs of its membership. The United States is eager to show its interest and promote its interests in Asia, the world's most dynamic region. Although some have claimed the world will break into three regional blocks, it is certainly not in the U.S. interest to concede Asia to Japan and to confine itself to the Americas. Japan similarly seeks to advance relations with its Asian neighbors, especially the ASEAN countries, but at the same time is

7. Panagariya (1993).
8. Young (1993).
9. Funabashi (1995).

eager not to alienate its most important ally, the United States. Indeed the presence of the United States also helps allay Asian concerns of Japanese domination. Japan is also supportive of an organization that includes the other NAFTA members and thus reduces the danger of a protectionist North American block. The smaller Asian nations are eager to avoid the dominance of any of the three giant economies: China, the United States, and Japan. Yet at the same time, the smaller economies want to involve the three giants in the region. China, which had difficulties joining the World Trade Organization, is eager to gain acceptance in the international trading system. Furthermore, in each economy important internal interest groups are eager to promote economic liberalization.

Someone has said, perhaps unfairly, that APEC is four adjectives in search of a noun. APEC members have agreed they are to form a "community." Although they have agreed what that does not mean, they are less clear on what it does mean. To help them decide, APEC enlisted an Eminent Persons Group to provide it with visions of what it might do. There is agreement that APEC will not be a community in the sense of a formal quasi-federal arrangement like the European Union, nor will it establish a large organization. Nor, certainly for the foreseeable future, will it be a customs union or a common market. Instead, APEC will promote trade and investment through a mix of policies that deal with trade liberalization, trade facilitation (initiatives that might include cooperation on standards, improving customs procedures, coordinating competition policies, and dispute mediation) and economic cooperation (development assistance and cooperation on projects in human resources, infrastructure, energy, and the environment).

Trade Liberalization

The most controversial issues in APEC relate to formal trade liberalization. APEC was promoted by several nations who are deeply committed to the multilateral trading system and concerned about the possibilities of a world divided into blocks that discriminate against outsiders. Thus while APEC is itself a regional arrangement, it has the paradoxical mission of combating (preferential) regionalism. Accordingly members have explored various ways in which regional liberalization can be open.

A key commitment to which all APEC members subscribed at the Bogor summit was to achieve free trade and investment in the region no later than 2020. Industrialized countries would proceed more rapidly and achieve such measures no later than 2010. This commitment presents both opportunities and risks. The opportunity lies in achieving improved access that moves beyond what is feasible through GATT or that eventually pushes the entire GATT toward full free trade. The risks lie in overpromising and thereby losing credibility. If nations in APEC could be convinced that the free trade goal will actually be attained, it would help allay some of the current concerns of participants on both sides of the Pacific. For example, many Asian countries are currently concerned about being shut out of the NAFTA market, but since both Canada and Mexico are part of APEC, an APEC free trade area would prevent this from happening. Similarly, some Asian nations are concerned that the United States could lose interest in the Pacific region, but again APEC's initiatives would help keep the United States involved. Several nations, including the United States, Australia, and New Zealand, are concerned that an exclusionary East Asian economic caucus could develop. Again the APEC arrangement and the agreement by Malaysia at Bogor to host a future summit meeting allayed some concerns. Similarly, China could see the declaration as indicating its acceptance into the world trading system.

Nonetheless, giving content to the free trade commitment will not be easy. Some countries resist the model of bargaining that has been typical of the give-and-take processes at GATT and other negotiations. A model of "concerted unilateral liberalization " has been put forward by some, suggesting that, instead, countries should act independently, each laying out its plans for multilateral liberalization and receiving encouragement and criticism from others.

This approach could in principle achieve an open region, with members eventually removing trade barriers to other members and to outsiders. But it faces problems relating to its credibility and the treatment of outsiders. If commitments are not serious and binding, others may be unwilling to reciprocate. Malaysia, for instance, has stressed that the Bogor commitment was hortatory rather than binding. A related problem is the treatment of outsiders. For small countries and those lacking in bargaining power, unilateral multilateral liberalization seems attractive. Such liberalization also appears advantageous to Japan, which is concerned about setting off a battle with Europe and, since it is seen as closed, is unable to use its market as a bargaining chip. But for a large country such as the United States, offering Europe and other non-APEC partners unconditional access without reciprocity is highly unlikely.

One alternative is to negotiate a conventional free trade agreement with a preset timetable for liberalization and a detailed outline of sectors to be covered.[10] This would make the agreement credible, but it might lock some countries into liberalization at a more rapid pace than they desired. It would also be difficult to make such an agreement nondiscriminatory. How might such an agreement be open? One way would be for APEC members to extend its free trade provisions to all countries that are prepared to reciprocate. Such a conditional most favored nation treatment might be more acceptable to the United States.

In the context of a traditional free trade area, the size of APEC has important political consequences. Notably GATT did not lay out an entire schedule to achieve world free trade at a single point in time. Instead, while members committed themselves to free trade as a long-term goal, they concentrated on making progress toward free trade in small steps. As might be expected, momentum was maintained by reducing barriers the most radically in sectors with the least political resistance. It was difficult, for example, to include agriculture in the system when farmers were a significant share of the population in developed countries. As their share diminished, change became easier. In practice, therefore, this approach allowed trade negotiators to choose the time they would take on domestic protectionist forces and build supporting coalitions.

10. Another alternative, explored by Wonnnacott (1994), is to remove all barriers in sectors in which APEC trade has a high share.

By contrast, a precise agreement with strict timetables to complete liberalization in all sectors, negotiated at one time, will force all the political battles to be fought at once. Consider, for example, the reactions of the farmers in Korea and Japan who would have to agree in principle that they are prepared to have complete free trade with Thailand and the United States; or the textile producers in the United States and Japan and Canada who would have to agree to complete free trade with China. In each APEC economy, there will be large alliances of the political opposition. It will be more difficult to find the countervailing group of supporters.

In contrast with APEC, other regional free trade agreements have been concluded between limited groups of countries. This arrangement allows members to alleviate the political difficulties of removing barriers in all sectors by offering producers the prospect of preferential access. But simultaneous liberalization within all of APEC would not allow this opportunity, even on a temporary basis. Given the size of APEC and the presence of world-class competitors in almost every industry, firms would find that extremely tough foreign competitors are being given equal access to other APEC markets. The virtue of the APEC approach, however, is that it places considerable pressure on countries not to be left out. Indeed, the larger the market, the greater the pressure.

In the United States, APEC free trade raises other concerns. One will be voiced by protectionists, who will not look kindly on the prospects of open competition with Asian nations such as China and Japan. Furthermore, as the debate about NAFTA made clear, many Americans are reluctant to grant free trade access to nondemocratic nations and those not respecting human rights (or freedom of the press). A third reason is that problems in trade with several Asian countries relate not to barriers at the border, such as tariffs that can be eliminated with a free trade agreement, but to domestic policies and regulations that close markets to outsiders. Although it is possible to imagine U.S. agreement with the more open Asian economies such as Hong Kong or Singapore, the prospects for a free trade area patterned after NAFTA between the United States and Pacific nations like Japan and Korea are much less likely. In Japan the "invisible barriers" presented by private sector practices that are officially allowed present more problems to American and other foreign firms than the formal rules that would be the subject of a free trade area arrangement. Accordingly, from an American standpoint, a free trade area with Japan would provide increased access for Japan to the U.S. market but would not necessarily provide reciprocal access for the United States. Only an agreement that included measures such as joint antitrust enforcement, mutual recognition of standards, and symmetrical market access and national treatment for foreign investors would deal with the central problems perceived in U.S.-Japan relations. For the United States, therefore, to make an APEC agreement politically acceptable, binding agreements on the issues that are labeled as trade facilitation would be important.

The Agenda for Deeper Integration

Besides its agenda for trade liberalization, APEC is simultaneously trying to launch several other projects. They include establishing a dispute mediation mechanism, achieving agreement on competition policies, common definitions of product standards and acceptance of testing results, and agreements on private investment. Monetary and macroeconomic cooperation and development and technical cooperation projects (dealing with human resources, tourism, and infrastructure and energy) have also been launched.

Many of these items come from the agenda for deeper integration rather than the traditional agenda of GATT. Some may be more feasible than the establishment of a formal free trade area. Indeed, APEC could be more successful in achieving deeper integration in some areas than in achieving shallow integration. Several of these issues have been promoted with great enthusiasm by the Pacific Business Forum, which was formed after the summit at Blake Island and which includes business representatives from throughout the APEC region.[11] Nonetheless, the first such agree-

11. The business leaders also presented a vision document that included calls for rapid liberalization of trade, a Pacific investment code, facilitation of customs procedures, the establishment of a businessman's visa, and establishment of a small and medium enterprise foundation.

ment, covering a code for foreign investment that was signed at Bogor, must be judged as highly disappointing. As Edward Graham emphasizes in his analysis, not only was the agreement not binding, it justifed investment-distorting practices rather than eliminating them.[12]

Open Regionalism

Besides facilitating the trade of APEC members, such projects and agreements could help make APEC markets more contestable for those outside the region. Success in concluding such agreements would therefore be a way of achieving regionalism that is open in a different sense. If regional arrangements go beyond border barriers and reflect agreements on domestic practices that reinforce market forces, they will make entry for outsiders easier and create rather than divert external trade. For example, harmonized regulations, more efficient customs procedures, or increased regulatory transparency would automatically help both insiders and outsiders in APEC. In many Asian countries interest in deregulation is growing. Some countries might find it easier to undertake these measures if they were part of an international agreement.

Besides engaging in free trade negotiations, Pacific nations could work out functional market-oriented programs at the regional level. These measures would include programs that improve the transparency and openness of regulatory practices, increase the speed with which nations move to adopt the intellectual property provisions in the Uruguay Round, and adopt rules that provide foreign-owned firms with national treatment on a nondiscriminatory basis. The Pacific nations could also make agreements on domestic deregulation that increase foreign access to financial and other regulated sectors, cooperate in enforcing competition policies, and place restraints on domestic agricultural subsidies. The successful conclusion of agreements in these areas would provide benefits that accrue automatically both within and beyond the region.

12. Graham (1994).

Nonetheless, as with formal trade agreements, achieving consensus in the form of binding agreements in these areas will not be easy. Agreements may be appropriate and attractive to some members and not to others. APEC's deeper integration menu is more likely to be *a la carte* than *prix fixe* and to proceed in a piecemeal fashion in coverage and membership.

Conclusion

GATT appears ideal to most Asian nations. In principle it provides access for nations on a most favored nation basis while at the same time permitting ample domestic policy autonomy. This presents an attractive trading environment, especially for Asian developing countries, which seek simultaneously to follow export-oriented policies while nurturing infant industries at home. Similarly, GATT presents a nation like Japan with opportunities to trade and yet at the same time the ability to develop unique domestic institutions. Many Asian countries are not in a strong political bargaining position.

Besides the problems I have just suggested they face in implementing a regional free trade area, therefore, both Japan and other Asian nations are understandably reluctant to implement any policy that would undermine the current multilateral system. Consequently most proponents of regional economic programs for Asian economies generally advocate some form of "open" regionalism. One approach would be for APEC nations to negotiate tariff reductions that would then be extended on a most favored nation basis to all trading partners. APEC's trading partners would undoubtedly welcome such an initiative, but some APEC nations themselves might find it hard to justify extending "free-rider" benefits to nations from outside the region. Moreover, while such an initiative would confer benefits on APEC consumers, it could also worsen the terms of trade for Asian products in global markets. Other obstacles to a formal free trade agreement reflect the diversity of APEC's members. In addition, political resistance to full liberalization in APEC will come from many quarters.

Regardless of whether progress toward formal free trade is made, APEC could help enhance the economic integration of its membership through agreements and projects that facilitate trade and investment. Paradoxically, perhaps, some in Asia seem to have concluded that although a free trade agreement is neither feasible nor desirable "the integration of measures not included in the GATT appear more attractive."[13] The aim would be to provide an environment in which goods, capital, labor, and information could move easily across borders. In the terms of this study, APEC's agenda would involve deeper rather than shallow integration.

13. Yamazawa (1993) argues that the harmonization of rules and the process of making national regulations transparent would encourage the enterprises of member and non-member countries to do business across the borders.

Chapter 8

Rules for Preferential Trading Arrangements

THE THEORETICAL MODELS of preferential trading arrangements do not establish unambiguously whether or not such arrangements improve global efficiency or lead to more multilateral liberalization. Nonetheless, as I argue in chapters 3 and 4, the models do indicate that the rules under which the arrangements are formed can greatly influence the outcome. These rules relate to external and internal tariffs and the compensation and accession of outsiders.

The GATT Rules

Article 24 of GATT stipulates when contracting parties may violate GATT's key principle of most favored nation treatment and form preferential trading arrangements such as customs unions and free trade areas. The basic notion behind Article 24 is that GATT will permit discrimination but only in return for full liberalization: the price of violating most favored nation should only be paid if countries are willing to go "all the way." GATT requires, therefore, that such agreements cover "substantially all trade." Furthermore, external tariffs should not be raised by countries concluding free trade areas, and in customs unions, the common tariffs of the group toward third countries should not "on the whole" be more restrictive than the "general incidence of" duties and regulations before the customs union was formed. The rules also allow these conditions to be met gradually. They allow

95

for "an interim agreement"—one that leads to a customs union or free trade area "within a reasonable time"—to depart from these provisions.[1] Agreements among developing countries are treated more leniently—basically they are free to establish whatever types of agreements they choose.[2] Finally, GATT requires countries to submit all agreements for examination by a working party to ensure conformity with GATT rules.[3] It is not necessary for agreements to be explicitly approved—they may be implemented unless the working party formally objects.

These GATT rules have been assailed from several directions. One concern is that they allow regional arrangements in the first place. Why not simply repeal Article 24? Responding to this question is useful because it reminds us how much liberalization has been achieved through regional arrangements, which are estimated to cover about 50 percent of world trade. How many countries would be willing to extend the tariff-free access they afford to their partners? History shows such a suggestion is impractical. If countries were required to practice complete most favored nation treatment today, they would undoubtedly seek to renegotiate the full array of their concessions. It is by no means clear that freer trade would result. Indeed it probably would not. Regional and preferential arrangements are therefore here to stay. So there is no substitute to having rules to constrain them.

A second line of criticism is focused on the agreement's rules, in particular the lack of theoretical rigor in the rules for substantially all trade to be covered and the requirement that countries not be compensated for trade diversion. A third concern is GATT's tolerance of both free trade areas and customs unions. A fourth is the lack of a constraint on accession for outsiders. A final concern relates to its inadequate enforcement of these rules. Let us evaluate these rules and the changes that have been proposed.

---

1. In the Uruguay Round the agreement states that "a reasonable length of time" should exceed ten years only in exceptional cases.

2. In 1979 these GATT provisions were further weakened in developing countries by the enabling clause that allows, in most cases, free trade areas that are agreed on between developing countries to bypass Article 24 altogether.

3. Although many agreements have been considered by GATT, few have actually been approved by a formal action by the parties.

"Substantially All Trade"

GATT requires that the parties eliminate barriers in "substantially all" trade. Does such a rule make sense? Pure trade theory would say, not necessarily, because it is quite possible that partially removing some internal barriers could be better than completely removing all of them. For example, if internal barriers are not removed in cases where there is trade diversion, global welfare would be higher than if such barriers are removed. Trade theory thus argues that eliminating internal barriers is likely to lead to lower welfare than would partially removing them.[4]

However, most of the trade theories assume that policymakers seek only to maximize national welfare. In reality decisionmakers may have political incentives to conclude agreements that promote the interests of some groups at the expense of others, and without the discipline of the GATT rule, trade diversion would probably be increased.[5] By requiring the removal of substantially *all* barriers, Article 24 prevents countries from framing agreements that maximize trade diversion and minimize internal adjustment by liberalizing trade only in products where members compete with outsiders rather than with one another. For example, assume Mexico makes no mainframe computers, but the United States and Japan do, while the United States makes no footwear, but Mexico and Korea do. An agreement between the United States and Mexico, which only liberalized trade in computers and footwear, would give U.S. producers an edge over their Japanese competitors in computers and Mexican producers an edge over Koreans in footwear. Such agreements are precisely the kinds of agreements that are likely to be negotiated when countries do not have the discipline of covering "substantially all trade" and when domestic firms have the ability to strongly influence outcomes.

---

4. As noted by Meade (1955, pp. 50–51) and Lipsey (1957) welfare is more likely to be raised if tariffs are merely reduced than if they are completely removed. The argument is that there is likely to be a second-best internal tariff rate that maximizes welfare. It could be above or below the current one. If it is above, and a nation makes a big move, welfare will clearly be reduced. If it is below and a nation makes a big move, it could move past it.

5. See Grossman and Helpman (1993).

This rule also reinforces the basic most favored nation principle of GATT by preventing countries from applying selective liberalization in just a few areas. For example, in the previous example, Mexico was willing to trade with the United States in computers duty free but not with Japan. GATT seeks to confine such arrangements to cases in which an intense political commitment is evidenced by the partners' willingness to make significant structural adjustments.

Finally, trading areas are the natural units of GATT. Once countries remove all internal barriers, they can legitimately be considered the equivalent of the nation-states that are the natural units for GATT. After all GATT membership initially reflects a world that historical accidents have divided into nation-states.

Maintain External Tariffs

GATT also places emphasis on not having tariffs raised by insisting that the formation of a preferential trade arrangement not be taken as an opportunity to renege on previous tariff bindings. In free trade areas, neither of the partners can raise its tariffs. When customs areas are formed, however, implementing this condition gives rise to problems. When the European Community was formed, for example, countries moved to the simple arithmetic average of the rates prevailing in each of the members. This decision raised average tariffs for Germany and Benelux and reduced them for Italy and France. Obviously some outsiders were helped, and others were hurt.

Again this rule is not clearly supported by trade theory. In particular it ignores the distinction between trade diversion and trade creation. As I described in chapter 3, the preferential treatment given to a partner in the agreement may reduce the demand for products from nonmembers even if external tariffs are not raised. However, GATT makes no mention of such trade diversion and ignores the impact such arrangements might have on outsiders even when they do not raise external tariffs.

One explanation for the GATT rules is that the signatories fail to understand this notion or are unwilling to confront powerful members with demands for compensation that GATT might be incapable of enforcing. Indeed the record of laxity with which GATT has enforced even its weaker conditions points to the problems it might face by demands for compensation for trade diversion.[6]

An alternative rule would eliminate trade diversion by insisting that preferential agreements leave outsiders at least as well off as they were before the agreement. This could be achieved by *lowering* external tariffs to maintain levels of imports from outsiders.[7] By eliminating the effects of trade diversion, this proposal would confine the effects of preferential agreements to trade creation and would also provide countries with an incentive to continue enlarging their agreements until all trading partners were included.

However, this prescription confronts both conceptual and practical problems. In principle, countries should know, prior to the agreement, what kind of compensation they would have to pay before entering an agreement. But, beforehand, there will inevitably be great uncertainty about the extent of trade diversion that is likely. Moreover, after the agreement comes into effect, separating the effects occurring because of the trade-diverting aspects of the agreement from other economic changes will be difficult. Indeed, the debates over the magnitudes of trade creation and trade diversion owing to the formation of the European Common Market remain today. A reduction in imports from the rest of the world does not necessarily indicate trade diversion. For example, diversion might not occur in the case of nontariff barriers being removed by an agreement. Assume that A is a more efficient producer than C, but that a quota originally constrained imports from A to B and thus B met its needs by buying from C. A free trade agreement between A and B that removed the quota would allow A to increase its sales at the expense of C, but this move would represent trade creation rather than diversion. The same would be true for many measures relating to behind-the-border barriers that increased

6. GATT has been extremely tolerant of special regional arrangements and never rejected one. According to Schott, GATT has never censured an agreement, and only four have formally been declared GATT-compatible. The experience with the EC is illustrative. The precursor to the EEC, the European Steel and Coal Community, clearly violated Article 24, but it was given a waiver by GATT.

7. See McMillan (1993) for such a proposal.

efficiency and thus improved the competitiveness of members of a preferential agreement.[8] Finally, preferential arrangements could have dynamic effects that enhance investment and growth. In the long run outsiders could therefore gain from imports induced by higher income even if in the short run they lost as a result of trade diversion.

In fact, therefore, given the impracticality of the alternative, the current GATT rule makes sense as a minimum restriction on new preferential agreements. The binding of tariffs is critical in imposing a discipline on the trading system. Some theories suggest there could be incentives for regional arrangements to become more protectionist. The binding of the external tariff provides an important constraint on such action.

Customs Unions and Free Trade Areas

Article 24 allows for both free trade areas and customs unions. Some have proposed that only customs unions be allowed. By concentrating on tariff barriers, the GATT rules miss a potentially powerful source of trade diversion that may occur when free trade areas are formed, namely, restrictive rules of origin.[9] Members of free trade areas differ in their external tariffs. They confront the problem that, without rules of origin, imports from outside the free trade area could be brought into the low-tariff countries and then shipped duty free to members with higher tariffs. Rules of origin that define eligibility for duty-free access for members of a free trade area provide an opportunity for raising barriers against outsiders while leaving tariff levels unchanged. Thus in NAFTA, for example, only apparel products that are 100 percent North American qualify for duty-free movement across NAFTA member countries. This creates a disincentive for the use of non-NAFTA fibers, yarn, and fabric.

Anne Krueger has argued that the rules of origin associated with free trade areas are likely to raise protection against outsiders. She

8. Another problem is that although the presumption is that its terms of trade will decline, as Corden has noted, possibly the rest of the world might have its terms of trade improved and thus not require compensation. Corden (1984).

9. Krueger (1995b).

also argues that the existence of rules of origin in which insiders are protected is likely to give firms a vested interest in maintaining protection and thus reduce the willingness of the free trade area to engage in external liberalization. This would suggest that only customs unions should be permitted by the GATT rules for preferential arrangements.[10] The problem with this prescription, however, is that countries concluding an agreement would lose the ability to conduct independent trade policies. Since many countries might be unwilling to give up this important dimension of sovereignty, this stricture might prevent free trade area agreements that are welfare enhancing. This requirement also ignores an important advantage of free trade areas—namely, that members can mitigate the harmful effect of trade diversion by lowering their barriers toward the outside world. Indeed, since trade diversion is harmful not only to outsiders but also to members of a free trade area, countries have an incentive to do precisely that.

Had such a rule been in effect, NAFTA would never have been concluded, since it is hard to imagine any of the three countries being willing to give up their trade policy independence. Moreover, despite the incentives that may exist for the United States to have tried to establish itself as the hub of a number of free trade agreements, it is noteworthy that Canada participated in NAFTA, and all three countries plan to negotiate the agreement's extension to Chile. Furthermore, the initiative for free trade in the Americas should help simplify the rules of origin.

Customs unions do have some important advantages. They avoid the crazy quilt complexity, expense, and inefficiency when countries join several free trade areas simultaneously. And even if rules of origin are not protectionist, their existence requires customs officials to inspect all products crossing the internal borders of a preferential arrangement.

But customs unions are not without their own problems when it comes to additional liberalization. Customs unions can increase

---

10. An even stricter rule than allowing only customs unions would be to allow only customs unions but to require that participants adopt the lowest tariff of any of the partners. This rule would lead to less trade diversion than the current rule, but it would also make countries with low tariffs less attractive partners.

the market power of their members. Indeed, the market power of the European Union is far greater than that of its members acting individually. Players with such bargaining power may see an advantage in using it to increase protection or to impose unilateral demands. As the discussion in chapter 5 on the EU has brought out, Europe has used such power in demanding voluntary restraint agreements and applying antidumping provisions. Indeed, NAFTA used the rules of origin as a protectionist tool of industrial policy (for example, the stipulation that certain processes must be performed in North America for televisions to qualify for duty-free treatment), but in a similar fashion the EU has used the requirement that semiconductors must have the diffusion process performed in Europe to escape antidumping actions.

The problem of rule of origin is an important one, but dealing with it through banning free trade agreements is too extreme a solution. It would surely be preferable to constrain free trade areas in their ability to tailor these rules to meet the protectionist demands of certain industries. One approach that would allow free trade areas to remain GATT-legal would be to permit only a single definition of local content to be used for all products. This would prevent definitions that are tailored to the protectionist interests of specific sections.

Open to Outsiders

A final suggestion would be to insist that all agreements be open to all outsiders willing to meet the conditions of the agreement. This would provide outsiders with a ready means for mitigating any trade diversion.

This approach, which has been put forward by the Eminent Persons Group as a proposal to achieve open regionalism in APEC, is attractive from an economic standpoint.[11] But especially as free trade agreements become increasingly intertwined with deeper economic integration, it becomes less feasible. It is hard to imagine how GATT could force agreements when partners were not will-

---

11. Eminent Persons (1994, p.175).

ing to do so, and not hard to imagine members defining conditions for access that inhibit outsiders from seeking to join.

Enforcement

A fundamental problem with prescriptions for tighter constraints on preferential agreements is that in practice GATT has not been effective in enforcing the ones contained in Article 24. Indeed, free trade agreements have invariably excluded agriculture and numerous other sectors and still have not been rejected by GATT. GATT has also not been strict in enforcing the rules relating to transition periods. Some agreements have such long periods for implementation that they can justify discriminatory treatment without full internal liberalization for extensive periods. Many agreements between developing countries have also not come close to meeting GATT rules.[12] This is unfortunate because failure to meet these rules can lead to agreements that are politically attractive but which increase trade diversion.

It was noteworthy that despite the widespread recognition that regional arrangements were increasing at the time the Uruguay Round was concluded, the rules for regional integration laid out in GATS (General Agreement on Trades and Services) were considerably weaker than those for GATT. In GATS no liberalization in services was required for an agreement to be acceptable—a simple standstill on existing measures was sufficient.[13] One explanation is that GATS has been worded with a view to ensuring that existing regional arrangements would be consistent with GATS. However, in GATT, countries are required to meet more demanding conditions of liberalization to qualify for preferential trading arrangements. The same should be true of GATS. Instead of drawing up

12. See Finger (1993); Schott (1989).

13. They must have "substantial sectoral coverage," a condition that is more lenient than "substantially all trade" for goods; second, they should eliminate existing discriminatory measures *or* prohibit new or more discriminatory provisions—in other words a mere standstill agreement may be sufficient. Third, such agreements are not to raise the overall level of barriers to trade in services originating in other GATS members within the respective sectors compared with the level maintained before the agreement. This description relies on Jackson, Davey, and Sykes (1995, p. 928).

rules that all existing agreements automatically meet, GATS should have grandfathered existing arrangements and adopted a rule requiring the listing of sectors that are not covered by liberalization. The negative list approach of NAFTA would have been far preferable since it would have made the restricted sectors apparent to all.

Strengthening GATT Rules and Enforcement

In my judgment, the major problems facing GATT are not in the specific rules of Article 24 governing goods. Instead they lie in problems in other GATT rules and in ensuring that the rules of Article 24 are enforced and apply to all members. The weak enforcement of Article 24 is symptomatic of the weakness in GATT enforcement more generally. Clearly reforms making GATT enforcement more effective and credible are required. In particular, working groups should take a far more active role in policing agreements. And agreements among developing countries should be brought under the same disciplines as those applied by developed countries.

The major abuses perpetrated by the emerging regional arrangements relate to their use of rules of origin and antidumping provisions. Both these sets of rules need to be reformed. First, the use of sector-specific rules of origin should be illegal. Only one rule should be allowed for all products for each member country (or free trade area). Second, the dumping rules need to radically restricted.

Chapter 9

Conclusion

*I*N THIS BOOK I have presented two contrasting views of regional or preferential trading arrangements. The traditional view focuses on the impact of tariff and nontariff liberalization, and analysts reach an ambivalent verdict because such arrangements both divert and create trade. Whether the proliferation of such arrangements undermines or increases the chances of achieving multilateral liberalization is also unsure.

Others acknowledge that some of these emerging preferential arrangements are broader and deeper than anything provided by the World Trade Organization (WTO). On the one hand, they liberalize investment and services more extensively; on the other, they promote efforts to adopt rules and governance in domestic policies that affect trade and investment. Once tariffs are removed, complex problems still remain, relating to different levels of subsidies and other industrial and regulatory policies. Traditionally, these policies are determined at the national level. Increasingly, however, globalization is creating pressures to reconcile divergent national practices through international agreement and governance. Indeed, there is no reason to assume that all public goods should be delivered by the nation-state. In some cases, the best outcome may be for groups of countries to provide such goods, either permanently or until a broader multilateral arrangement can be concluded. In principle, some regional arrangements may well be first best.

I have also surveyed the emerging regional arrangements that include the major industrial nations. This survey offers support for the notion that the newer arrangements are dealing with measures that have not been dealt with by GATT. Some opponents of these regional arrangements see the "deeper" integrative aspects of these arrangements as pernicious and undesirable. They view them as mechanisms for foisting inappropriate rules and restraints on weaker, smaller, and in particular, developing countries.

Jagdish Bhagwati, a free trade opponent of regional arrangements, views them as "a process by which a hegemonic power seeks (and often manages) to satisfy its multiple trade-unrelated demands on other, weaker trading nations more easily than through multilateralism." Free trade arrangements seriously damage the multilateral trade liberalization process by facilitating the capture of it by extraneous demands that aim, not to reduce trade barriers, but to increase them as when market access is sought to be denied on grounds such as "eco-dumping" and "social-dumping."[1]

In negotiations between countries with differing market sizes, an asymmetrical power relationship will probably exist. However, this unevenness does not mean that poor, small countries will lose in these associations. Indeed, the power asymmetries reflect the fact that the gains, especially those from realizing scale economies, are likely to be relatively larger for the smaller country. Similarly, economic integration generally leads to convergence, with poorer economies growing more rapidly than richer economies. Moreover, small countries join these agreements voluntarily. Indeed, if NAFTA or the Canada-U.S. Free Trade Agreement had been seen as U.S. initiatives, they would have been doomed politically from the start. In both cases, the governments and firms of these countries saw these agreements as in their own interests and did not participate simply because they feared American protectionism. The same is true of the east European nations that are voluntarily seeking to join the European Union and those in Latin America seeking a hemispheric arrangement with the United States.

Moreover, while countries seeking to join these arrangements may have to make "concessions" by adopting some rules and institutions that may not suit their needs perfectly, they also enjoy

1. See, for example, Bhagwati and Krueger (1995, pp. 13–14); Perroni and Whalley (1994).

benefits from adopting institutions without having to go through the costs of developing them. Just as several European countries have sought to import the credibility in fighting inflation enjoyed by the Bundesbank by pegging their exchange rate to the German mark, so countries can make their regulatory policies more credible through international cooperation. As I described in chapter 2, many aspects of these agreements help make international trade and investment more efficient and international competition more intense, yielding dynamic benefits to all participants.

Clearly, the emerging regional arrangements vary radically in scope, depth, and governance mechanisms.[2] Although most aim at liberalization of trade in goods and services, they differ significantly in their reliance on sectoral exceptions, the degree of coordination of trade policy, the degree to which they harmonize domestic policies, and how much they liberalize capital and labor movements and cede national sovereignty to supranational bodies.

In all these respects, the European Community has clearly proceeded the furthest. The EC is characterized by strong measures to achieve the complete integration of national markets for goods, services, capital, and labor; a common external trade policy; measures to harmonize and or mutually recognize domestic policies; and supranational legislative, judicial, and executive institutions.

The EC 92 initiative focused heavily on how domestic policies helped create obstacles to a single market. This initiative turned to non-trade-related policies such as incompatible technical standards, public health inspections, government procurement rules, taxation, corporate law, labor regulations, subsidies, transport regulation, and competition policy.

The Canada-U.S. agreement moved beyond GATT to only a limited degree. U.S. investment in Canada was not fully freed. There were many exceptions to the liberalization of services, and agricultural subsidies were not dealt with. Although some constraints were placed on Canadian energy policies, more generally, no constraints were placed on industrial policies. Measures to

2. This section draws heavily on de la Torre and Kelly (1992).

reconcile different standards and provide national treatment for government procurement were modest at best. All in all, the agreement is more accurately thought of as a traditional free trade agreement with some coverage of services.

NAFTA is a more extensive agreement. It is noteworthy for the absence of sectoral exceptions in goods trade (besides Canadian agriculture), the broader treatment of services, the extensive liberalization of investment, obligations on intellectual property rights that exceed those in the WTO, and the remarkable fact that this agreement was reached between nations at dramatically different levels of economic development. NAFTA and its side agreements provide for trinational oversight of national practices, but NAFTA does not include common rules for government subsidies and competition policies. As a result, members continue to apply their own rules for dumping and countervailing duties. Nor, it should be stressed, did the side agreements change labor or environmental standards in each NAFTA country. All these agreements did was to provide for international oversight of enforcement.

Deeper regional arrangements mean sharing sovereignty. It is fascinating to see the varied ways in which nations in the EU and NAFTA have tried to accomplish this objective. For instance, international rules can be internationally enforced, as the EU does with its competition policies. Or countries can adopt national policies that are accepted internationally, as occurs with mutual recognition in the EU. Countries may make an international agreement on policies but enforce them nationally, as stipulated in NAFTA's intellectual property rules. Finally, international oversight of national policies may occur, as exemplified by the NAFTA appeals process.

Despite the commitment by the members of the Asia-Pacific Economic Cooperation forum to achieve free and open trade no later than 2020, many questions remain about whether a formal free trade area in the Asia-Pacific region is likely. Several Asian economies are intent on avoiding measures that are discriminatory. One approach would be to develop their regional trading and investment links informally and to use the APEC organization to achieve some measures of deeper integration where Asians can move beyond GATT.

The EU and NAFTA offer important lessons on the effects that deeper regional arrangements could have on the global trading system. Deeper is not necessarily better or worse. The nature of the policies that have been implemented is more important than whether or not such policies are harmonized. When the EU has adopted highly interventionist approaches, most notably in the Common Agricultural Policy, it has greatly undermined progress toward a more liberal global agricultural trade system. The adoption by the EU as a whole of the protectionist nontariff barriers of its members has similarly restrained global trade. By contrast, the use of market-oriented measures, such as the harmonization and mutual recognition of standards and restraints on state aids imposed by its common competition policy, has resulted in more open EC markets and the development of mechanisms that could be emulated more widely. Similarly, when NAFTA has reinforced liberalization and deregulation, especially in Mexico, it has meant a more open economy for competitors from outside the arrangement. Arrangements that move toward deep integration along free market lines are likely, simultaneously, to increase the access of outsiders. Such arrangements should therefore be encouraged to expand their membership and to move beyond the measures that can be achieved by GATT. On the other hand, arrangements stifling market pressures can hurt outsiders and should be resisted.

Are the current regional arrangements building blocks or stumbling blocks? Two features are critical in determining the answer. First, the motives leading countries to form these agreements are generally not protectionist. To be sure, sometimes the preferential aspects of the agreements are attractive to domestic interests, but these agreements are being signed by developed and developing countries that are liberalizing unilaterally and in the WTO.

The members of the European Common Market simultaneously lowered their internal and external trade barriers. Having privatized many state-owned firms and liberalized its external trade, the Salinas administration used NAFTA to reinforce its policies and to make them visible, credible, and permanent. By guaranteeing access for its producers to the U.S. market, Mexico became a more attractive location for foreign investment, not to serve the domestic market behind high barriers but to serve all North American markets by employing Mexican labor. Both the United States and Canada not only liberalized regionally through NAFTA, they also did so multilaterally, in the WTO.

Second, the agreements have been open to enlargement. Both the desire to be part of a thriving arrangement and the need to minimize the effects of trade and investment diversion exert strong pressures on nearby countries to join successful regional agreements. The key to broader arrangements is successful smaller arrangements. The experience of other agreements indicates that successful regional arrangements place strong gravitational forces on bordering countries and create incentives for expansion. This is clearly the lesson of the European Union, which began with just six nations, expanded to become twelve, and now includes fifteen. Nations inevitably compete with their neighbors in goods and factor markets. There is a strong need, therefore, for neighbors outside an arrangement to match the producer benefits that derive from membership. Thus nations throughout the Western Hemisphere agreed in Miami in December 1994 to extend NAFTA and to achieve free trade in the Western Hemisphere by 2005, and the nations of eastern Europe seek to join the European Union.

Regionalism is here to stay. Keeping these arrangments open is the key issue, and the WTO has an important role to play in doing so.

The major risk in the evolving regional arrangements is that they could implement new forms of protection, not by erecting new tariffs but by implementing rules of origin and administering antidumping and countervailing duties that have protectionist effects.

Although the rules of GATT may have deficiencies, no alternative offered has been without problems. Instead, the GATT procedures for overseeing that the rules are implemented need to be strengthened. Members should not be allowed to adopt sector-specific rules of origin, and the antidumping rules should be reformed. Eventually these rules should be replaced by an international competition policy. Until agreement is reached, however, only the price discrimination definition of dumping should be allowed, and the methods by which the differential is measured should be tightly constrained.

Comments

Louka T. Katseli

This is an interesting and insightful paper on a very topical but underresearched subject. Since the mid-1980s, more than sixty regional economic arrangements (RAs) have been negotiated among countries across all five continents. The most well known include the European Internal Market (EC 92) and its subsequent evolution toward a European Economic and Monetary Union (EMU), the conclusion of the North American Free Trade Agreement (NAFTA), and finally the launching of a major regional initiative in the Pacific (APEC), in parallel with an agreement to implement an ASEAN Free Trade Area (AFTA) by the year 2007.

The central question that Robert Lawrence poses is whether these RAs are "stumbling or building blocks toward a more integrated and successful international economy." To answer this question, Lawrence investigates, theoretically and empirically, the characteristics of the emerging RAS to conclude the following:

—The current initiatives are generally the outcome of pro-trade and investment strategies by transnational companies (TNCs), rather than the outcome of import-substitution policies by nation-states.

—Present-day RAs, especially in Europe, represent "deeper" as opposed to "shallower" forms of integration, involving not only

Louka T. Katseli is professor of economics at the University of Athens.

111

the removal of tariffs and other trade barriers but also the reconcil-
iation of divergent national practices and regulatory policies.

—Deeper integration gives rise to a whole set of "collective
goods" for the participating members, including not only common
standards, competition rules, fixed currencies or environmental
and labor policies but also enhanced credibility for domestic policy
initiatives, secure access to enlarged markets, large-market externalities, and so on.

—In the context of globalization of economic activity, supranational and subnational regionalism are responses to a diminished role of the nation-state as a provider of public goods;
although the existence of scale economies and the international-
ization of production tends to increase the scope of governance,
the growing tendency to match diversified needs and choices
leads to its localization.

—No clear theoretical case can be made on the likely effects of
preferential arrangements on the process of multilateral liberalization; instead, political and economic factors, such as the relative
power of internal protectionist interests, the diversion of political
capital, the relative power of outsiders demanding accession, and
other circumstances are important determinants of that process.

Given the ambiguous effects of RAs on multilateral liberalization and the wide differences in scope, depth, and governance
across existing RAs, substantiated by the three case studies presented, Robert Lawrence concludes that the central policy problem is not the eligibility of RAs under GATT, but rather the
weakness of GATT's enforcement rules, which, in turn, need to be
strengthened.

Furthermore, Lawrence argues in favor of an international competition policy, banning sector-specific rules of origin and reforming antidumping rules, and he supports multilateral agreements
for deeper RAs, so as to spread the benefits of such action more
equitably across countries.

In presenting his argument, the author chooses to answer a
much more limited question than the one posed at the beginning
of his book. He, thus, focuses his analysis explicitly on the effects
of RAs on the prospects of multilateral liberalization, rather than

on the "integration and successful functioning" of the international economy. In so doing, he limits his scope to more traditional trade-based concerns, despite his early warning that present-day RAs are motivated by the desire to facilitate international investment in goods and services and to develop regional production systems.

Even though multilateral liberalization is a necessary condition for the integration and success of the international economy, it is clearly not a sufficient condition. In the global order of today, which is underpinned by massive capital movements carried through by TNCs, as well as by the rapid development, use, and diffusion of new technologies and by the sizable knowledge transfers undertaken through investment flows, much of worldwide competition centers around the availability of capital for development and the access that domestic enterprises have to the "insider networks" established by TNCs.[1] As the study notes, Mexico's interest in joining NAFTA stemmed from its determination to secure access to its major trading partners' market and thus to persuade investors to use it as an export platform. Similarly, RAs in Asia are formed with a view toward enhancing investment and enabling firms, on the one hand, to integrate their production regionally and, on the other, to service both the regional and global markets.

It is the presence of these substantial large or thick-market externalities from the formation and the functioning of investment-led RAs, rather than the degree of their openness to trade, that poses the danger of creating a "fractured world order" characterized by "insiders and outsiders."[2]

In light of such considerations, an evaluation of the impact of present-day RAs on the functioning of the international economy should consider, besides trade effects, such factors as the following:

—The distribution of foreign direct investment (FDI) induced by RAs that could lead to an asymmetric concentration of capital and to capital shortages in nonparticipating countries.

1. Katseli (1993).
2. Segasti (1990).

—The potential deterioration of relative profitability of firms that are systematically excluded from sourcing, production, or marketing networks facilitated by RAs.

—The evolution of structural competitiveness of insiders relative to outsiders, owing to differences in their access to entrepreneurial or technological know-how.

—Positive and/or negative externalities associated with the supranational governance spurred by RAs. Finally,

—The optimality of the mix and sequencing of policies adopted by aspiring members in their efforts to converge quickly toward RA norms.

In that light, note that between 1988 and 1992, following the Single European Act that formally launched the European Internal Market process (1992), the stock of FDI into Europe increased from 36.5 percent of the world stock to 43 percent. The corresponding share for all developing countries remained unchanged at 21.6 percent, largely because of the channeling of increased FDI toward a few countries in Asia.[3] At the same time, the concentration of FDI flows toward a few developing countries increased further. The ten largest host countries increased their share of FDI from 68 percent of the total inflows to developing countries to 76 percent.[4]

Given these trends, it would be interesting to analyze how much of this investment reallocation and concentration can be attributed to the formation and deepening of RAs and to evaluate the effects of these developments on the integration and real convergence of the world economy.

These negative investment effects, if they in fact exist, could then be contrasted with what seem to be positive trade effects of RAs since, at least in Europe, total trade with developing countries appears to have expanded considerably between 1988 and 1994.[5] These trade effects seem consistent with the author's stipulation

3. United Nations (1994).
4. United Nations (1994, table 1.5).
5. Between 1988 and 1994, European Union exports to developing countries increased from 16.9 per cent to 21.2 percent of total exports. The corresponding import share rose from 17.8 percent to 20.8 percent. IMF (1995, p. 78).

that the deepening of RAs tends to be associated with positive dynamic trade effects, but further empirical research is needed to explore the pattern of causality between them.

The European experience with deeper integration is also a good test case for the dynamic effects of RAs on outsiders' relative competitiveness. If the investment-diversion effects of deep RAs are indeed significant, then, this is expected to have negative effects on the productivity and competitiveness of nonparticipating members. The same could be said with reference to technological or managerial capabilities, which are more likely to be developed and contained within the internal networks of TNCs in the course of entrenchment of regional home-market positions.

Finally, as the European experience has shown, aspiring candidates for accession often tend to streamline their own policies to those of insiders, regardless of important structural or institutional differences, of the optimal sequencing of domestic liberalization, or of the negative effects of such policies on domestic living standards. Thus many central and eastern European countries undertake exchange-rate and monetary policies with an eye to gaining credibility in their quest for an early integration with the European Union, rather than in accordance with domestic restructuring or growth objectives. The same could be said for some of the less developed countries within the European Union (Greece, Spain, Portugal, or Ireland), which pay a high price in terms of employment and growth for the purpose of adhering to nominal convergence criteria. That they are wiling to do so suggests that RAs generate political and economic benefits that outweigh costs and that these advantages go much beyond the usual trade-creation effects one associates with the customs-union literature. These dynamic gains to insiders, associated among other things with enhanced credibility, thick-market externalities, access to sourcing and marketing networks, preferential access to technology, and managerial know-how can be considered dynamic losses to outsiders.

These considerations pertain to deeper forms of integration, which, as Lawrence notes insightfully, signify "a change in the world institutional order."

It would be interesting to explore, in that light, whether present-day RAs such as NAFTA, which is characterized by the author as a "GATT-plus agreement") or APEC, which goes beyond GATT in many respects, are likely to proceed further with deeper forms of integration.

The European experience suggests that this is likely for several reasons. From a business point of view, FDI in goods and services is facilitated by common practices and rules between the home and host countries; hence, the pressure to create a "single market" or a "unified economic area." From both a business and a financial point of view, the free movement of capital is supported by the minimization of exchange rate risks; hence the move toward fixed exchange rates and the coordination of monetary policies that could eventually lead to monetary integration. This process in turn requires some fiscal discipline among participating members and some convergence of their fiscal policies, as well as the institution of a regional transfer system to ease the burden of adjustment, to compensate losers, and to ensure the political viability of the RA. As a result, despite repeated recourse to subsidiarity principles, the role of the nation-state as a provider of public goods is eroded.

Finally, the transfer of important economic decisions at the supranational level increases the pressure for the evolution of supranational institutions that would guarantee adequate democratic representation of all actors and would safeguard the necessary political accountability of the system; hence economic and financial integration is likely to strengthen supranational governance, bring about the formation of some regional institutions, and lead to some degree of political integration.

The internal dynamics of this process of deepening, which eventually brings about monetary and institutional integration, is likely to put limits to enlargement. The trade-off between deepening and enlargement, which has dominated the public debate in Europe, is thus likely to become pertinent in other continents as well. This would run counter to Lawrence's trade-based intuition that "if regional arrangements go beyond border barriers and reflect agreements on domestic practices that reinforce market forces, they will make entry for outsiders easier and create rather than divert external trade."

From a policy perspective, the answer to this dilemma might lie with "flexible regional arrangements" as suggested by Mathias and others for the European case.[6] According to their view, an integration process is effective and flexible when all participating members accept some fundamental rules, but then individual countries are free to form deeper partnerships on selected issues. This concept can be applied at the global level. All countries can conclude multilateral agreements, which, as the author suggests, safeguard open trade, strengthen the enforcement procedures of GATT, and extend them to cover services and to ensure the liberalization of such sensitive sectors as agriculture. Furthermore, agreements on the rules of conduct for foreign investment and on an international competition policy should be pursued at the global level in order to minimize the detrimental structural effects of deeply integrated RAs on outsiders. Finally, if RAs are not to develop into "closed clubs," some "entry rules" or "free-access safeguards" could be multilaterally established.

In the context of such a level global playing field, countries can then be free to participate in RAs and to deepen their cooperation and integration on various economic, social, or political spheres with minimum danger for international cohesion.

The discussion so far has been based on the presumption, made by the author as well, that RAs are here to stay. One could argue, however, that RAs are going to be more "footloose" than one expects, since TNCs are likely to shift the location of production at the global level and to develop new sourcing, trade, or investment networks that cut across continents and present-day RAs in accordance with their corporate strategies. In such a world order, RAs, which represent deeper forms of integration, are likely to become costly and suboptimal forms of international organization. In other words, if one expects RAs to be transitory arrangements owing to economic fundamentals, then, it becomes even more important to avoid deeper forms of regional integration and to maintain institu-

---

6. Mathias and others (1995).

tional flexibility. In that case, what is needed along with the policy guidelines suggested above, is the strengthening and reform of global institutions. They in turn could develop their own regional governance structures to match the regional requirements of the marketplace. This view strengthens the argument for flexible and open regional arrangements. They should be embedded on a set of extended and reformed multilateral agreements and institutions, which ensure, through proper enforcement, the successful functioning of the international economy.

Yung Chul Park

This is a comprehensive survey of trade theories and experiences with preferential trading arrangements (PTAs) and regional economic arrangements (REAs). More important, Robert Lawrence also presents interesting new insights into the formation of current REAs, whether they are structured as customs unions or as free trade areas (FTA). It is not clear, however, whether this study is going to help settle the controversy over the role of REAs in strengthening the multilateral trading system. Depending on how Lawrence's arguments are interpreted, one could become optimistic or pessimistic about the role the expansion of regionalism will play in promoting a more integrated world economy.

Lawrence's main thesis is that neither traditional trade theory nor past experience is useful in understanding the driving forces behind the formation of current REAs. In his view, the two most prominent REAs, the European Union (EU) and the North American Free Trade Agreement (NAFTA), are responses to a demand for deeper integration: the need to provide a number of public goods—such as standards, competition rules, common currencies, and environmental and labor policies—at a regional level. This demand has arisen from economic globalization, which has brought about a massive increase in foreign direct investment and trade in services.

According to Lawrence, motives leading many small, as well as large, countries to form REAs are in general not protectionist, and most of the current REAs are open to enlargement. For these reasons, he seems positive about the role of REAs in achieving multilateral free trade. However, his painstaking examination of theories about REAs does not establish whether they would, in fact, be more conducive to multilateral trade liberalization. The outcome is more sensitive to the rules under which REAs are created—and these are related to their external and internal tariffs and accession policies. Thus, the question of whether REAs will weaken or strengthen incentives for multilateral free trade is an empirical one.

Yung Chul Park is professor of economics at Korea University and president of Korea Institute of Finance.

Is there credible evidence to back Lawrence's optimistic view? Lawrence's review of the experiences of the EU, NAFTA, and the Asia-Pacific Economic Cooperation forum (APEC) does not throw much light on the matter. In my view, developments both in Europe and North America cast doubt on whether REAs will be building blocs for a multilateral free trade system.

Fred Bergsten suggests that Europe and North America have become more inward looking in the 1990s.[1] The Clinton administration has shown little interest in any new trade initiatives. Chile's accession to NAFTA is simply avoided, and U.S. enthusiasm for APEC-wide trade liberalization was noticeably lacking at the Osaka summit in 1995. Membership in the EU has increased to sixteen, but it is not clear whether members are interested in adding countries outside Europe.

At this stage how realistic is it for the EU or NAFTA to enter serious negotiations for mergers with REAs on a one-to-one basis? Because of the closed nature of both the EU and NAFTA, many small PTAs have sprung up around the world. In 1995 the World Trade Organization (WTO) received notification of twelve new REA agreements. During the past five years, a remarkable forty-five new arrangements have come into existence. During the same period, twenty-five new nation-states (most from the former Eastern bloc) became members of the United Nations. What implications do these new nations have for the future of the WTO-based multilateral trading system and also for REAs?

The variety of ways in which partners in the EU and NAFTA have tried to share sovereignty impresses Lawrence very much. Member countries of an REA seem prepared to give up some autonomy, at least to the extent that doing so is beneficial to them economically. However, countries draw a clear line between integration of their economies and surrendering autonomy in the political or military spheres. Nation-states, particularly those that have been colonies or dominated by a powerful regional hegemony, can be very nationalistic. It is thus difficult to imagine how there can be deeper integration within current and prospective

---

1. Bergsten (1996).

REAs. Even in Europe, the prospects for further monetary and political integration look much less certain than a few years ago.

Lawrence's central thesis—that the current initiatives in forming REAs originated in globalization of the world economy—is not disputed. However, whether the emergence of a number of closely integrated REAs will be supportive of multilateral free trade is a totally different question. It may be true that globalization is the driving force behind integration with REAs—that is, the growing need to harmonize internal rules and policies at a regional level—but to establish any erodible causality between deeper integration on the one hand and multilateral free trade on the other, it is necessary to define an optimal region or group of countries for which some of the public goods could be produced more efficiently. Lawrence fails to do so.

Indeed, REAs could be first-best as providers of many public goods, but it is not enough to say that the available technology of public goods production and diversity of consumer choice are factors determining the structure, the geographical area, and the number of members of a particular REA. This question is important because economic globalization cannot explain the recent proliferation of REAs. Technology for the production of public goods and consumer tastes change and converge over time. Unless the economic and political determinants of the REA are more clearly identified, the future of REAs is quite unpredictable.

If integration with REAs continues, some of the large REAs could become regional fixtures of the world trading system, competing for a larger share of markets and, in the process, ending up with managed trade among and even within themselves. Surely, the current move toward REAs in many cases has little to do with efficient production of public goods at the regional level. Instead it is no more than an attempt to improve bargaining positions in comparison with larger REAs.

Lawrence's central thesis also ignores the problem arising from the overlapping of REAs, in particular overlapping FTAs, which suggests that current FTAs are likely to erode support for the open, multilateral trading system. Anne Krueger argues that there is no uniform way of setting rules of origin, comparable to concepts such as uniform tariffs.[2] This point is important because rules of origin determine the tariff structure applied to a trading partner in an FTA. Thus negotiations must take place on new rules of origin for each applicant to join an FTA. The problems associated with rules of origin in one FTA are troublesome enough, and they are bound to become more complex when FTAs overlap. Indeed, if more and more FTAs are established with complex rules of origin, further accessions are not a straightforward matter. And at the end of the process membership of all and an open, multilateral trading world may not be the result.

Finally, Lawrence stresses the importance of achieving multilaterally deeper integration between countries so that smaller countries are not forced to accept inappropriate rules by joining REAs. Paradoxically, however, deeper integration of current and future REAs will make it harder to achieve deeper integration at a multilateral level and lead REAs to become stumbling blocs rather than building blocs for multilateral free trade in the future. Suppose there are a large number of REAs, and some of them are more influential than others, but all are intent on succeeding in harmonizing regional rules and policies. In the dynamic real world, the development of communication and transportation technologies, globalization of information and knowledge, and increasingly freer movements of factors of production all change in unpredictable ways. Thus the appropriate or optimal region or group of countries for which a set of public goods can be produced most efficiently can also change. In the future, therefore, many current REAs—especially smaller ones—will not survive as viable entities economically or politically. They will have to merge with other REAs and even be absorbed into larger ones. Such a development may be desirable from an efficiency point of view, but if REAs are somewhat deeply integrated, they will find merging more difficult and face more serious political opposition to the merger than otherwise. Shallowly integrated REAs will have a much easier time than the deeply integrated ones, and they will face less resistance when they merge with other arrangements or even integrate into a larger REA.

2. Krueger (1995c).

In reality, most current REAs have loose structures and are no more than political alliances designed to increase market power and bargaining position in their attempt to join larger, more powerful, REAs. Because of their shallow integration, mergers between small REAs and the enlargement of larger REAs such as NAFTA will be easier than otherwise. To the extent that the EU and NAFTA remain the key trading blocs and are reluctant to accommodate new members, however, small REAs and small countries will have incentives to form additional REAs.[3] They will also find it in their interest to forge strategic alliances with other REAs to counter the dominant position of the dominant REAs. If small countries form new REAs and alliances between REAs continue to shift as expected, for all practical purposes the WTO will be represented by REAs rather than by individual countries. Within such an organization, the decision-making process will be greatly influenced by the dominant REAs and by how alliances between REAs are formed. It is indeed an open question whether such a change in the decision-making process in the WTO will be conducive to developing a liberal, multilateral trading system. Indeed, if the proliferation of REAs is left unchecked, the idea of imperial harmonization or a tripolar system may not be so farfetched. Perhaps the open regionalism espoused by APEC members is, after all, the best way of halting the aimless drift into a world littered with many competing REAs.

In the final analysis, whether current REAs will contribute to building an integrated world trading system remains uncertain. In any case, as Lawrence argues, the REAs are here to stay, so we might as well keep them open. In this regard, he says the WTO has an important role to play because it is the only forum where some of the rules—such as the rules of origin and antidumping rules that have been abused by large REAs—can be reformed. However, in view of the proliferation of REAs, which is likely to alter the WTO's decisionmaking process, it is not clear whether the WTO will indeed be the viable alternative.

3. Park and Yoo (1989).

Appendix

Table A-1. *Selected Regional Trading Arrangements: General Framework*

Name	Membership	Dates	Broad objectives
Africa			
UDEAC (Central African Customs and Economic Union)	Cameroon, Central African Republic, Chad, the Congo, Equatorial Guinea, Gabon	Signed in 1964 Effective in 1966 1994: Signed treaty establishing the Economic and Monetary Community of Central Africa	Common market: implementation of common external tariff, replacement of quantitative restrictions (QRs) with tariffs, and phased elimination of intra-area duties; harmonization of policies. Member countries are also members of the franc zone and share a common currency as well as a common central bank.
Asia			
AFTA (ASEAN Free Trade Agreement)	Brunei Darussalam, Indonesia, Malaysia, Philippines, Singapore, Thailand	Established in 1992	Free trade area to be achieved by 2008. Goal of 0–5 percent preferential tariff on manufactured goods and elimination of QRs. Regional industrial cooperation. This agreement is still in an early stage of development.
ANZCERTA (Australia–New Zealand Closer Economic Relations Trade Agreement)	Australia, New Zealand	Signed in 1983 Modified in 1988	Free trade area: harmonization of business law and cooperation in the area of standards and customs procedures. Elimination of antidumping within the FTA.
APEC (Forum for Asia-Pacific Economic Cooperation)	Australia, Brunei, Canada, Chile, China, Hong Kong, Indonesia, Japan, Malaysia, Mexico, New Zealand, Papua New Guinea, Philippines, Singapore, South Korea, Taiwan, Thailand, United States	Established in 1989 1994: Bogor Declaration	Promotion of consultation and cooperation for regional economic development. Facilitation of trade through harmonization of regulations and standards. Draft free trade agreement that aims for "open regionalism" and free trade and investment in the region by 2010 for industrialized nations and by 2020 for developing countries (on MFN basis).

EAEC (East Asian Economic Caucus)	Brunei, China, Hong Kong, Indonesia, Japan, Republic of Korea, Malaysia, Philippines, Singapore, Taiwan Province of China, Thailand	1990	Economic cooperation: regional consultative forum designed to represent members' views in global and regional negotiations and to expand regional cooperation. To date, the EAEC's political agenda has dominated its economic agenda.

Europe

EEA (European Economic Area)	Twelve member states of the EU and seven countries of the EFTA (see lists below)	Signed on May 2, 1992 Entered into force in 1994	Free trade area: the free movement of goods, persons, services, and capital within the whole EEA as well as broadened cooperation in horizontal policies. Establishment of common rules and equal conditions of competition and adequate means of enforcement (including at the judicial level). Adoption of EC law by EFTA countries (excluding issues of monetary cooperation, tax harmonization, foreign, economic, and defense policy). No common external tariff.
EU (European Union)	Belgium, Denmark, France, Germany, Greece, Ireland, Italy, Luxembourg, Netherlands, Portugal, Spain, United Kingdom (Austria, Finland, Norway, and Sweden are expected to accede in 1995 pending referendums)	1957: Treaty of Rome 1992: Single European Act establishing Internal Market 1992: Maastricht Treaty	Customs union: economic and monetary union to be achieved by 1997 or 1999 at the latest (will be one of the largest internal markets in goods and services in the world). Coordination of fiscal and socioeconomic policies. Approximation of rules in areas of intellectual property rights and industrial property rights. Efforts to improve functioning of internal market, especially in terms of better rule enforcement and faster incorporation of EU rules into national legislation.

Table A-1. (continued)

Name	Membership	Dates	Broad objectives
EFTA (European Free Trade Association)	Austria, Finland, Iceland, Liechtenstein, Norway, Sweden, Switzerland	Formed in 1960	Free trade area: free trade among countries that did not join EU for political or economic reasons. Currently negotiating agreements with central and east European countries.
Latin America			
ANCOM (Andean Common Market)	Bolivia, Colombia, Ecuador, Peru, Venezuela	Andean Pact established in 1969 with Cartagena Declaration. Revived in 1990 with Acta de la Paz.	Common market: customs union to be achieved by 1995. Recently agreed on common external tariff with preference to other Latin American countries. Harmonization of social and economic policies. Recent agreement to improve intellectual property protection. Many member countries have signed bilateral free trade agreements with other nations and trade groups in the Western Hemisphere (including the United States).
CARICOM (Caribbean Community)	Antigua and Barbuda, Bahamas, Barbados, Belize, San Cristobal, Dominica, Grenada, Guyana, Jamaica, Montserrat, St. Kitts and Nevis, St. Lucia, St. Vincent and the Grenadines, Trinidad and Tobago	Established in 1973	Common Market: Phasing down of the common external tariff to reach a 5–20 percent range by 1998.
MERCOSUR (Southern Cone Common Market)	Argentina, Brazil, Paraguay, Uruguay	Signed in 1991 (Treaty of Asuncion)	Common Market by 1995. Coordination of fiscal, foreign exchange, and customs policies. Free movement of goods, services, capital, and labor throughout the region through elimination of tariffs and NTBs, establishment of common external tariff, coordination of macroeconomic policy, and harmonization of internal legislation as needed.

Middle East			
GCC (Gulf Cooperation Council)	Bahrain, Kuwait, Oman, Qatar, Saudi Arabia, United Arab Emirates	Established in 1981	Common market: Achievement of integration among member countries through free movement of goods, services, and factors of production.
North America			
CUSFTA (Canada-U.S. Free Trade Agreement)	Canada, United States	Signed in 1988	Free trade Area: tariff liberalization for trade in goods within five to ten years. Some harmonization of technical standards; some liberalization of government procurement.
NAFTA (North American Free Trade Agreement)	Canada, Mexico, United States	Signed in 1992 Effective January 1, 1994	Free trade area: phased reduction of tariffs and quotas in goods and services. Substantial liberalization of investment flows. Side agreements on labor, environment, and import surge protection. Establishment of intellectual property right protection.

Sources: Anderson and Blackhurst (1993); Bollard and Mayes (1992); de la Torre and Kelly (1992); de Melo and Panagariya (1993); Gibb and Michalak (1994); Hufbauer and Schott (1993, 1994, 1995); IMF (1993, 1994); Satoshi Isaka, "Seeking Free Trade, APEC Must Now Get Down to Details," *Nikkei Weekly*, June 25, 1995; Kewalram (1994); Nobuyuki Oishi, "Japan's APEC Initiative Shifts Focus," *Nikkei Weekly*, February 13, 1995; Reinisch (1993).

Table A-2. Selected Regional Trading Arrangements: Reduction of Border Barriers

Name	Goods	Investment	Services	Labor
Africa				
UDEAC	Historically, there has been almost complete nonimplementation of intra-area liberalization. However, a new tariff reform program is to be implemented by 1995 (common external tariff with four rates will replace all customs duties, taxes and levies; intra-area tariffs will be eliminated over next five years). QRs will be eliminated over three-year period.	Members share a common code for investment policy.	...	...
Asia				
AFTA	Schedule of tariff cuts over a fifteen-year period, beginning in 1994. First-stage cuts tariffs by 20 percent within five to eight years; second stage lowers tariffs to 0.5% in following seven to ten years. Eventual elimination of QRs. Phase-out of NTBs over five years from initial concessions on an item.	Investment is not covered under agreement.	Services are not included in the agreement.	...

ANZCERTA	All tariffs and QRs have been removed in a series of annual steps over the years 1983–90 (five years ahead of schedule).	Capital movement between two countries was already relatively free when agreement was signed.	Since 1990, most intra-area trade in services is free of tariffs. Some exemptions remain (agreement broke new ground by establishing negative list of services specifically excluded by each country.)	Labor was already very mobile between two countries before agreement was signed.
APEC	Discussion regarding nature of tariff reductions will take place in November 1995.	Exploratory work has been undertaken to review members' investment regimes and to increase transparency.	Discussion on liberalization of services will take place in November 1995.	...
EAEC	...	...	...	...
Europe				
EEA	Provisions for trade in goods are largely identical to those of the EC treaty. Agricultural and fishery products are not included.	Provisions for investment are largely identical to those of the EC treaty.	Guarantees freedom to provide services for all nationals of any EEA state to anyone in another EEA state. Includes special provisions that prohibit national rules having discriminatory effect on EEA transport carriers.	Adoption of EC law that abolishes nationality-based restrictions on economic activity of workers and self-employed persons.
EU	Since 1992, most intra-area trade in manufactures is free of tariffs and QRs. Some sector-specific internal quotas remain, however. (Voluntary export restraints in agriculture, textiles, and clothing, autos, and consumer electronics).	All restrictions have been lifted from the movement of portfolio capital among members. Provisions have been made for firms' freedom of establishment (new firms), but members still favor bids from domestic firms for takeovers.	Most tariffs and QRs have been removed with the exception of energy, telecomms, and transportation. Exceptions are also made for leasing services, legal services, accountancy, and postal services).	Labor movement is almost completely liberalized (difficulties remain with nonprofessional refugees). Barriers exist in form of professional and vocational qualifications and limited portability of fringe benefits, pensions, and so on.

Table A-2. (*continued*)

Name	Goods	Investment	Services	Labor
EFTA	All tariffs on manufactures eliminated by 1967. QRs eliminated by late 1970s. Common external tariff exists (not harmonized with that of EU).	...	...	Provisions for free labor mobility exist only within the Nordic countries.
Latin America				
ANCOM	Elimination of tariff barriers to intra-area trade in almost all products (except capital goods). Four-tier common external tariff to be implemented beginning in 1995 (with some exceptions).	In 1991 previously restrictive foreign investment rules were reformed, and national treatment was provided to foreign investors.	...	Free movement of labor has not yet been achieved. However, members have agreed to coordinate their approach to educational issues (including professional certification, recognition of credentials, and so on).
CARICOM	Most intra-regional trade has been liberalized. First phase of common external tariff (brings tariff rates down to 0–35 percent) was implemented starting in January 1993, after many delays (smaller countries have consistently postponed adoption of the external tariff).	Systems of Rules for Enterprises is a pact that promotes investment in certain sectors.	...	Some progress has been made in facilitating the free movement of labor within the region, largely through integration of the educational system (including regional examinations).

MERCOSUR	Countries must apply progressive and automatic schedule of intraregional tariff reduction steps to be completed by end of 1994. NTBs to be eliminated by same date. (Paraguay and Uruguay have an extra year to implement agreement). A common external tariff has been agreed upon for 85 percent of products. No common external tariff on capital goods and high-technology products.	Substantial restrictions impede the free movement of capital, although reforms have been undertaken by Argentina and Brazil to encourage foreign investment.	. . .	Agreement provides for free movement of people by 1995. Travel within region has been facilitated substantially (passport is not required).
Middle East GCC	Virtual elimination of all customs tariffs by 1982. Unification of tariff schedules by 1983. Implementation of common external tariff between 4 percent and 20 percent. Special exception granted to Oman, which can levy tariffs on some products from within region. Near elimination of QRs.	Capital markets of GCC members are fully integrated. Citizens of member countries are allowed to purchase and own shares of industrial companies in all member countries and can borrow from special financial institutions providing industrial development loans.	Liberalization of trade in services by 1983.	Liberalization of trade in skilled labor; professionals of member countries can register and practice in any other member country.

Table A-2. (*continued*)

Name	Goods	Investment	Services	Labor
North America				
CUSFTA	Ten-year phase-out of tariffs (by 1998) including textiles, apparel, petro-chemicals, and steel. Prohibition of a number of QRs. Agriculture only partially liberalized. Some exclusions.	Some degree of preferential access for U.S. investors in Canada but exclusion of financial services, transportation, Crown corps, and investment related to govt. procurement.	Positive list of services to be liberalized, notably financial services (also computer-based services, tourism, architecture, and professional labor services).	Provisions were made to liberalize trade in some professional labor services (managerial and technical employees and entertainers).
NAFTA	Five- to ten-year phase-out of all tariffs (fifteen years in sensitive sectors). Liberalization of NTBs. Elimination of tariffs and quotas on textiles, apparel, and cars. Free trade in agricultural products within fifteen years.	National treatment for member investors. Mexican export perfor-mance, local content, and foreign exchange requirements are being phased out. Reduction of taxes on dividends, interest, and royalties. Some restrictions remain in Mexico's basic energy and railroad industries, Canada's cultural industries and U.S. airline and radio industries.	Substantially opens up financial services in Mexico to United States and Canada by 2000 (includes phased reduction of tariffs and NTBs in banking, insurance, and brokerage sectors). Nearly full liberalization of telecomm and land transportation services. Establishment of negative list of exceptions.	Includes provisions for entry of business and professional personnel. Intra-company transferees are allowed to enter member countries. 5,500 additional Mexican professionals are allowed to enter United States annually (above global immigration limits).

Sources: See table A-1.

Table A-3. *Selected Regional Trading Arrangements: Remaining Impediments*

Name	Rules of origin	Antidumping provisions (versus Competition Policy)	Subsidies	Sectoral exceptions
Africa				
UDEAC	...	...	...	Many domestic industries remain protected despite the new trade liberalization effort.
Asia				
AFTA	At least 40 percent of a product's content must originate from a member state.	...	...	Services are excluded from the agreement. Also excluded are raw agricultural products, mineral fuels, and motor vehicles. Member states have right to temporarily exclude sensitive items.
ANZCERTA	At least 50 percent of a product's value must be attributable to raw materials or value added from within the region. Last process performed in manufacture of good must take place in a member state.	Antidumping measures were eliminated in 1990. Replaced by competition policy.	All subsidies on intra-area exports were eliminated in 1990. Industry assistance (which has been substantial in the past) is now being eliminated.	A few agricultural subsectors remain protected in Australia.
APEC	n.a.	n.a.	n.a.	n.a.
EAEC	...	...	...	...

Table A-3 (continued)

Name	Rules of origin	Antidumping provisions (versus Competition Policy)	Subsidies	Sectoral exceptions
Europe				
EEA	Aims to improve EC rules of origin.	Establishment of common legal framework for competition; adoption of EC competition law on EEA-wide scale. No common antidumping policy.	Far-reaching prohibition on granting state aid that distorts EEA-wide competition.	Agricultural and fishery products; energy and telecomms.
EU	Yes	Antidumping measures were eliminated within area, but common antidumping policy exists. Establishment of strong competition policy and enforcement mechanisms covering trade among members.	European competition policies have reduced state aid, but level of subsidization is still high. Communitywide subsidy for agricultural products (CAP).	Within community: energy, telecomm, and transportation. Community-wide external tariff on agricultural products (CAP), coal, steel, and shipbuilding.
EFTA	...	...	Agricultural products are heavily subsidized at the national level.	Intra-area trade in agricultural products has not been liberalized.
Latin America				
ANCOM	...	...	...	Exceptions include petrochemicals, iron and steel, leather and textile products. Each country's list of exceptions should be eliminated by 1995.
CARICOM	...	...	...	...
MERCOSUR	Assembled products must have minimum of 40 percent domestic value added. Rules of origin will no longer be in force after implementation of common external tariff.	Common legislation on antidumping and countervailing duties entered into force in 1994.	...	Members submitted substantial list of products to be excluded from agreement. These lists have been progressively reduced and should reach zero by the end of 1995 (includes agricultural products and selected sectors of heavy industry).

Middle East				
GCC	At least 40 percent of value added must be produced within region, and at least 51 percent of the capital of producing firm must be owned by citizens of member countries.	. . .	. . .	Oman has been granted the right to levy tariffs on products from within the region.
North America				
CUSFTA	Product must undergo change in tariff heading (CTH) or must involve 50 percent value-added from a member country in order to be deemed to originate in that country.	Continued application of existing antidumping and countervailing laws to trade within FTA.	Farm subsidies remain in existence in both countries. Commitment to phase out subsidies in automotive sector.	Investment in Canada's cultural industries and U.S. airline and radio industries is limited to domestic investors. Telecomm, transportation, medical and legal services, and child care were excluded from agreement.
NAFTA	Highly restrictive rules of origin in autos, textiles, and apparel, and computers.	Continued application of antidumping laws, but Mexican procedures have been brought closer to those of United States and Canada.	No progress made in eliminating subsidies.	Foreign investment is restricted in Canada's cultural industries, Mexico's basic energy and railroads, and U.S. airlines and radio.

Sources: See table A-1.

n.a. Not available.

Table A-4. *Selected Regional Trading Arrangements: Moves toward Deeper Integration (Governance)*

Name	Regulations and standards	Government procurement	Dispute settlement	Supranational institutions
Africa				
UDEAC	Reforms have been implemented to simplify the fiscal system and unify customs procedures.	...	...	...
Asia				
AFTA	...	...	...	...
ANZCERTA	Explicit commitments to harmonize business laws, customs procedures, state government purchasing, and technical standards. Similarities in competition policies and legal systems already existed as did some harmonization in intellectual property and consumer protection laws.	Mutual preferences in public procurement practices (between Australia and New Zealand).	...	None
APEC	Expressed intent to harmonize product standards, customs regulations, and other administrative procedures.	n.a.	n.a.	n.a.
EAEC	...	...	...	...

Europe			
EEA	Focuses on elimination of technical trade barriers by harmonizing technical regulations, standards, testing requirements, and certifications.	Adoption of EC directive; mandates EEA-wide transparent public notice system for procurement exceeding certain threshold value.	A variety of different judicial, political, and quasi-judicial systems exists with some overlapping of jurisdictions. No EEA Court.	EEA Council (main political organ); EEA Joint Committee (administrative and legislative body); EEA Arbitration Tribunal; European Surveillance Authority (supervises competition policy); EFTA Court of Justice
EU[a]	Mutual recognition of each country's regulations and standards (includes firms' rights of establishment and certification of professionals) unless minimum communitywide standards have been set (in health, safety, environment). Aim to abolish all customs formalities. Some differences in technical standards and indirect taxation persist. Working on harmonization of technical product standards.	Public procurement of goods and services has been made subject to rules providing for transparency and free market access. Some monitoring problems exist.	Disputes are handled by the Court of Justice.	Commission (administrative and technical body); Council of Ministers (main decisionmaking body); Court of Justice (enforcement of common body of law); and the Assembly (parliament). Each of these organizations has power that is comparable to institutions in federal states.
EFTA	Different technical standards persist. Some efforts to harmonize standards with the EU.	Provisions to reduce discrimination in government procurement.	. . .	Court of Justice: implements community law.

Table A-4 *(continued)*

Name	Regulations and standards	Government procurement	Dispute settlement	Supranational institutions
Latin America				
ANCOM	...	...	...	The Justice Tribunal of the Cartagena Agreement; the Andean Parliament (supervises political aspects of agreement); Andean Council (to guide process of economic integration and political cooperation). However, these organizations have not yet performed their assigned functions.
CARICOM	...	...	...	The Caribbean Development Bank and several regional technical organizations including the Caribbean Environmental Health Institute, the Caribbean Regional Drug Testing Laboratory, and the Caribbean Meterological Organization. Opposition to creation of a Caricom Commission.
MERCOSUR	Countries have agreed to attempt to harmonize some regulations and standards.	...	Dispute settlement mechanism modeled on that of CUSTFA. Provides for quick resolution of disputes by arbitration panel. In addition, a special dispute resolution procedure for disputes arising during transition to common market.	Common Market Council supervises implementation and operation of agreement. Common Market Group oversees ten working groups on trade, regulatory, and macroeconomic issues among members.

Middle East

GCC	Steps have been taken to harmonize certain prices throughout the region, including telephone rates, water rates, and prices of petroleum products.	GCC companies are granted a 10 percent preferential margin in government contracts.	…
			…

North America

CUSFTA	No new procedures to reconcile differences in standards and regulations. Some recognition of each country's testing. Promotion of harmonization of standards.	Some efforts have been made to reduce discrimination in government procurement.	Establishment of innovative procedures to deal with bilateral disputes arising from antidumping and countervailing duty cases. Decisions subject to binding review by binational panel.	U.S.-Canadian trade commission that administers dispute settlement procedure.
NAFTA	No common set of rules or institutional harmonization. Enforcement of domestic laws is subject to international scrutiny.	Liberalization of procurement by major government agencies in all three countries.	Disputes handled by Free Trade Commission (augments dispute settlement provisions of CUSFTA).	Free Trade Commission: supervises implementation of agreement, resolves disputes; Commission for Environmental Cooperation: commits members to improve and enforce domestic environmental protection laws; Commission for Labor Cooperation: forum for consultation on domestic labor standards. In addition, eight committees and six working groups on various trade issues.

Sources: See table A-1.

n.a. Not available.

a. The EU has entered into association agreements with several central and east European countries; partnership agreements with several countries of the former USSR; free trade agreements with Baltic countries; customs union with Turkey and is in the process of negotiating agreements with some Mediterranean countries.

Table A-5. *The Bogor Declaration, November 1994*

At the Bogor summit, Bogor, Indonesia, all eighteen members of the Asia-Pacific Economic Cooperation forum agreed to "the long-term goal of free trade and investment" in the Asia-Pacific region by 2010 for industrialized nations and by 2020 for developing economies. The Bogor Declaration represents a broad commitment and does not detail the steps by which the members will achieve this goal. Similarly, there is no mention of which countries must meet the earlier target date. Nevertheless this group will probably include the United States, Canada, Japan, Australia, and New Zealand. Singapore and Taiwan have volunteered to liberalize by 2010 as well.

There is some disagreement among the APEC members over the precise goals of the organization: should APEC aim to turn the region into a free trade area similar to NAFTA, or should the group remain a largely consultative body? Some members, notably the United States and Australia, have advocated the setting of a timetable for trade and investment liberalization, while others, such as Malaysia and China, prefer that each country be allowed to open up at its own pace. Japan has expressed the view that peer pressure rather than a strict schedule is a more appropriate motivation for this particular group of countries, especially given that they are all at very different stages of economic development. Japan is also interested in using APEC as a forum to promote coordination on issues central to regional economic development such as the improvement of infrastructure and human capital as well as technology transfer within the region.

The next meeting of the APEC leaders took place in Osaka, Japan, in November of 1995. As host of the meeting, Japan was charged with preparing an "action agenda" to achieve the goals adopted at the Bogor summit.

References

Anderson, Kym, and Richard Blackhurst, eds. 1993. *Regional Integration and the Global Trading System*. London: Harvester Wheatsheaf for the GATT Secretariat.

Bagwell, Kyle, and Robert W. Staiger. 1993a. *Multilateral Tariff Cooperation during the Formation of Customs Unions*. Working Paper 4543. Cambridge, Mass.: National Bureau of Economic Research (November).

———. 1993b. *Multilateral Tariff Cooperation during the Formation of Regional Free Trade Areas*. Working Paper 4364. Cambridge, Mass.: National Bureau of Economic Research (May).

Baldwin, Richard. 1989. "The Growth Effects of 1992." *Economic Policy* (October): 248–81.

———. 1993. *A Domino Theory of Regionalism*. Working Paper 4465. Cambridge, Mass.: National Bureau of Economic Research.

Bergsten, Fred. 1996. "The Case for APEC: An Asian Push for World-wide Free Trade for APEC." *Economist*, January 6–12:62–63.

Bhagwati, Jagdish. 1992. "Trading Choices: The Americas or the World?" Columbia University.

———. 1994a. Comment on Hoekman in *The New GATT: Implications for the United States*, edited by Susan M. Collins and Barry P. Bosworth, 111–17. Brookings.

———. 1994b. "The Demand to Reduce Diversity among Trading Nations." Columbia University. Mimeo.

Bhagwati, Jagdish, and Anne O. Krueger. 1995. *The Dangerous Drift to Preferential Trade Agreements*. Washington: American Enterprise Institute for Public Policy Research.

Bollard, Alan, and David Mayes. 1992. "Regionalism and the Pacific Rim." *Journal of Common Market Studies* 30 (June): 195.

Bosworth, Barry, and Gur Ofer. 1995. *Reforming Planned Economies in an Integrating World Economy*. Brookings.

Brown, Drusilla K. 1992. "The Impact of a North American Free Trade Area: Applied General Equilibrium Models." In *North American Free Trade: Assessing the Impact*, edited by Nora Lustig, Barry Bosworth, and Robert Z. Lawrence, 26–68. Brookings.

Bryant, Ralph C. 1995. *International Coordination of National Stabilization Policies.* Brookings.

Casella, Alessandra. 1993. *Trade as an Engine of Political Change: A Parable.* Discussion Paper 779. London: Centre for Economic Policy Research.

Cecchini, Paolo, with Michel Catinat and Alex Jacquemin. 1988. *The European Challenge, 1992: The Benefits of a Single Market.* Aldershot, Hants, England: Gower.

Chia, Siow Yue, and Tsao Yuan Lee. 1993. "Subregional Economic Zones: A New Motive Force in Asia-Pacific Development." In *Pacific Dynamism and the International Economic System,* edited by C. Fred Bergsten and Marcus Noland, 225–72. Washington: Institute for International Economics.

Collins, Susan, and Dani Rodrik. 1991. *Eastern Europe and the Soviet Union in the World Economy.* Washington: Institute for International Economics.

Collins, Susan M., and Barry P. Bosworth, eds. 1994. *The New GATT: Implications for the United States.* Brookings.

Cooper, C. A., and B. G. Massell. 1965. "A New Look at Customs Union Theory." *Economic Journal* 75 (December): 742–47.

Cooperation, United States National Committee for Pacific Economic. 1995. *Pacific Economic Outlook 1995–6.* Pacific Economic Cooperation Council.

Corden, W. Max. 1972. "Economies of Scale and Customs Union Theory." *Journal of Political Economy* 80 (May-June): 465–75.

———. 1984. "The Normative Theory of International Trade." In *Handbook of International Economics,* vol. 1, edited by Ronald W. Jones and Peter B. Kenen, 63–130. Amsterdam: North Holland.

Cox, David, and Richard G. Harris. 1986. "A Quantitative Assessment of the Economic Impact on Canada of Sectoral Free Trade with the United States." *Canadian Journal of Economics* 19 (August): 377–94.

de la Torre, Augusto, and Margaret R. Kelly. 1992. *Regional Trade Arrangements.* Occasional Paper 93. Washington: International Monetary Fund (March).

de Melo, Jaime, and Arvind Panagariya, eds. 1993. *New Dimensions in Regional Integration.* Cambridge University Press.

Deardorff, Alan V. 1993. "Should Patent Protection Be Extended to All Developing Countries?" In *The Multilateral Trading System: Analysis and Options for Change,* edited by Robert M. Stern, 435–48. University of Michigan Press.

Deardorff, Alan V., and Robert M. Stern. 1991. "Multilateral Trade Negotiations and Preferential Trading Arrangements." In *Analytical and Negotiating Issues in the Global Trading System,* edited by Alan V. Deardorff and Robert M. Stern, 27–85. University of Michigan Press.

Doern, G. Bruce, and Brian W. Tomlin. 1991. *Faith and Fear: The Free Trade Story.* Toronto: Stoddart.

Drysdale, Peter, and Ross Garnaut. 1993. "The Pacific: An Application of a General Theory of Economic Integration." In *Pacific Dynamism and the International Economic System,* edited by C. Fred Bergsten and Marcus Noland, 183–224. Washington: Institute for International Economics.

Eichengreen, Barry J. 1995. *International Monetary Arrangements for the 21st Century.* Brookings.

Eminent Persons Group. 1994. "Achieving the APEC Vision: Free and Open Trade in the Asia Pacific." 94-EP-01. Singapore: APEC Secretariat.

Encarnation, Dennis J. 1992. *Rivals beyond Trade: America versus Japan in Global Competition.* Cornell University Press.

Finger, J. Michael. 1993. "GATT's Influence on Regional Arrangements." In *New Dimensions in Regional Integration,* edited by Jaime de Melo and Arvind Panagariya, 128–55. Cambridge University Press.

Fishlow, Albert, and Stephan Haggard. 1992. *The United States and the Regionalisation of the World Economy.* Paris: OECD Development Centre.

Flamm, Harry. 1992. "Product Markets and 1992: Full Integration, Large Gains?" *Journal of Economic Perspectives* 6 (Fall): 7–30.

Frankel, Jeffrey A. 1993. "Is Japan Creating a Yen Bloc in East Asia and the Pacific?" edited by Jeffrey Frankel and Miles Kahler, 53–85. University of Chicago Press.

———. 1996. *Does Regionalism Undermine Multilateral Trade Liberalization or Support It? A Political Economy Survey.* In *Regional Trading Blocs,* chap. 10. Washington: Institute for International Economics. Forthcoming.

Frankel, Jeffrey A., Ernesto Stein, and Wei Shang-jin. 1993. *Trading Blocs: The Natural, the Unnatural and the Super-Natural.* University of California. Mimeo.

Fukasaku, Kiichiro. 1992. *Economic Regionalisation and Intra-Industry Trade: Pacific-Asian Perspectives.* Technical Papers 53. Paris: OECD Development Centre.

Funabishi, Yoichi. 1995. *Asia Pacific Fusion: Japan's Role in APEC.* Washington: Institute for International Economics.

Gasiorek, Michael, Alasdair Smith, and Anthony J. Venables. 1992. *1992: Trade and Welfare—A General Equilibrium Model.* Discussion Paper 672. London: Centre for Economic Policy Research.

Gestrin, Michael R., and Alan M. Rugman. 1995. *The NAFTA Investment Provisions: Prototype for Multilateral Investment Rules?* Paris: OECD Trade Directorate.

Gibb, Richard, and Wieslaw Michalak, eds. 1994. *Continental Trading Blocs: The Growth of Regionalism in the World Economy.* John Wiley and Sons.

Graham, Edward M. 1994. "Towards an Asia Pacific Investment Code." Working Paper 94-2. Washington: Institute for International Economics.

Grossman, Gene, and Elhanan Helpman. 1993. *The Politics of Free Trade Agreements.* Working Paper 4597. Cambridge, Mass.: National Bureau of Economic Research (December).

Haaland, Jan I. 1993. *Welfare Effects of '1992': A General Equilibrium Assessment for EC and EFTA Countries.* Discussion Paper 828. London: Centre for Economic Policy Research.

Haggard, Stephan. 1995. *Developing Nations and the Politics of Global Integration.* Brookings.

Hazlewood, Arthur. 1979. "The End of the East African Community: What Are the Lessons for Regional Integration Schemes?" *Journal of Common Market Studies* 18 (September): 40–58.

Helpman, Elhanan and Paul R. Krugman. 1985. *Market Structure and Foreign Trade: Increasing Returns, Imperfect Competition, and the International Economy.* MIT Press.

Hoekman, Bernard M., and Petros C. Mavroidis. 1994. *Linking Competition and Trade Policies in Central and East European Countries.* Discussion Paper 1009. London: Centre for Economic Policy Research.

Hoekman, Bernard M. 1992. "Regional versus Multilateral Liberalization of Trade in Services." Discussion Paper 749. London: Centre for Economic Policy Research.

Hufbauer, Gary Clyde, ed. 1990. *Europe 1992: An American Perspective.* Brookings.

Hufbauer, Gary Clyde, and Jeffery J. Schott. 1992. *North American Free Trade: Issues and Recommendations.* Washington: Institute for International Economics.

———. 1993. *NAFTA: An Assessment.* Washington: Institute for International Economics.

———. 1994. *Western Hemisphere Economic Integration.* Washington: Institute for International Economics.

———. 1995. "Toward Free Trade and Investment in the Asia-Pacific." *Washington Quarterly* 18 (Summer): 37.

Inter-American Development Bank. 1995. *Economic Integration in the Americas.* Washington.

International Monetary Fund. 1993. *World Economic Outlook.* Washington.

———. 1994. *International Trade Policies: The Uruguay Round and Beyond. Volume II. Background Papers.* Washington.

———. 1995. *Direction of Trade Statistics,* world and area tables. Washington.

Jackson, John H., William J. Davey, and Alan O. Sykes, Jr. 1995. *Legal Problems of International Economic Relations: Cases, Materials and Text on the National and International Regulation of Transnational Economic Relations.* St. Paul, Minn: West Publishing.

Jacquemin, Alexis, and André Sapir, eds. 1989. *The European Internal Market: Trade and Competition.* Oxford University Press.

Jacquemin, Alexis, and André Sapir. 1991. "Europe Post-1992: Internal and External Liberalization." *American Economic Review* 81 (May): 166–70.

Japan, Industrial Structure Council of. 1995. *The WTO Consistency of Trade Policies.* Tokyo: Research Institute of International Trade and Industry.

Johnson, Harry G. 1958. "Optimum Tariffs and Retaliation." In *International Trade and Economic Growth: Studies in Pure Theory,* edited by Harry G. Johnson, 31–61. London: George Allen and Unwin.

Johnson, Harry G. 1987. "Optimal Trade Intervention in the Presence of Domestic Distortions." In *International Trade: Selected Readings,* edited by Jagdish N. Bhagwati, 235–63. MIT Press.

Katseli, Louka T. 1992. *Foreign Direct Investment and Trade Interlinkages in the 1990s: Experience and Prospects of Developing Countries.* Discussion Paper 687. London: Centre for Economic Policy Research.

Katseli, Louka, T. 1993. *Foreign Investment and Trade Linkages in Developing Countries.* ST/CTC/154. New York: United Nations (April).

Kemp, Murray C., and Henry Y. Wan, Jr. 1976. "An Elementary Proposition Concerning the Formation of Customs Unions." *Journal of International Economics* 6 (February): 95–97.

Kewalram, Ravi P. 1994. "EU: The Australia-New Zealand Closer Economic Relations Trade Agreement." *Reuter Textline* (February 25).

Kowalczyk, Carsten, and Tomas Sjostrom. 1993. *Bringing GATT into the Core.* Working Paper 4343. Cambridge, Mass.: National Bureau of Economic Research.

Kowalczyk, Carsten, and Ronald J. Wonnacott. 1992. *Hubs and Spokes, and Free Trade in the Americas.* Working Paper 4198. Cambridge, Mass.: National Bureau of Economic Research (October).

Krueger, Anne O. 1993a. "American Bilateral Trading Arrangements and East Asian Interests." In *Trade and Protectionism,* edited by Takatoshi Ito and Anne O. Krueger, 25–44. University of Chicago Press.

———. 1993b. *Free Trade Agreements as Protectionist Devices: Rules of Origin..*Working Paper 4352. Cambridge, Mass.: National Bureau of Economic Research (April).

———. 1995a. *Trade Policies and Developing Nations.* Brookings.

———. 1995b. "NAFTA: Strengthening or Weakening the International Trading System?" In *The Dangerous Drift to Preferential Trade Agreements,* edited by Jagdish Bhagwati and Anne O. Krueger, 19–33. Washington: American Enterprise Institute for Public Policy Research.

———. 1995c. "Problems with Overlapping Free Trade Areas." Paper presented at the National Bureau of Economic Research Sixth Annual East Asian Seminar on Economics, Seoul, Korea. (June).

Krugman, Paul R. 1991a. "Is Bilateralism Bad?" In *International Trade and Trade Policy,* edited by Elhanan Helpman and Asaf Razin, 9–23. MIT Press.

———. 1991b. "The Move toward Free Trade Zones." In *Policy Implications of Trade and Currency Zones.* A Symposium sponsored by the Federal Reserve Bank of Kansas City. Jackson Hole, Wyoming.

Langhammer, Rolf J. 1992. "The Developing Countries and Regionalism." *Journal of Common Market Studies* 30 (June): 211–31.

Laredo, Armando Toledano. 1992. "The EEA Agreement: An Overall View." *Common Market Law Review* 29 (December): 1199–1213.

Lawrence, Robert Z. 1991. *An Analysis of Japanese Trade with Developing Countries.* Discussion Paper 87. Brookings.

———. 1993. "Trends in World Trade and Foreign Direct Investment." In *South Africa and the World Economy in the 1990s,* edited by Pauline H. Baker, Alex Boraine, and Warren Krafchik, 2–31. Brookings.

Lawrence, Robert Z., Albert Bressand, and Takatoshi Ito. 1996. *A Vision for the World Economy: Openness, Diversity, and Cohesion.* Brookings.

Lawrence, Robert Z., and Charles L. Schultze, eds. 1987. *Barriers to European Growth: A Transatlantic View.* Brookings.

Lincoln, Edward J. 1992. *Japan's Rapidly Emerging Strategy toward Asia.* Technical Paper 58. Paris: OECD Development Centre.

Lipsey, Richard G. 1957. "The Theory of Customs Unions: Trade Diversion and Welfare." *Economica* 24 (February): 40–46.

Lipsey, Richard G., and Kelvin Lancaster. 1956. "The General Theory of Second Best." *Review of Economic Studies* 24: 11–32.

Lipsey, Richard G., and Murray G. Smith. 1989. "The Canada-US Free Trade Agreement: Special Case or Wave of the Future?" In *Free Trade Areas and U.S.*

Trade Policy, edited by Jeffery J. Schott, 317–36. Washington: Institute for International Economics.

Lustig, Nora, Barry Bosworth, and Robert Z. Lawrence, eds. 1992. *North American Free Trade: Assessing the Impact.* Brookings.

Mathias, M., and others. 1995. *Flexible Integration: Towards a More Effective and Democratic Europe.* CEPR MEI 6. London: Centre for Economic Policy Research (November).

McKinnon, Ronald I. 1963. "Optimum Currency Areas." *American Economic Review* 53 (September): 717–24.

McMillan, John. 1993. "Does Regional Integration Foster Open Trade? Economic Theory and GATT's Article XXIV." In *Regional Integration and the Global Trading System,* edited by Kym Anderson and Richard Blackhurst, 292–310. St. Martin's Press.

Meade, James E. 1955. *The Theory of Customs Unions.* Amsterdam: North Holland.

Mundell, Robert A. 1961. "A Theory of Optimum Currency Areas." *American Economic Review* 51 (September): 657–64.

Mundell, Robert A. 1964. "Tariff Preferences and the Terms of Trade." *The Manchester School of Economic and Social Studies* 32: 1–13.

Nicolaidis, Kalypso. 1989 . "Mutual Recognition: The New Frontier of Multilateralism?" *Project Promethee Perspectives* (June): 21–34.

Norberg, Sven. 1992. "The Agreement on European Economic Area." *Common Market Law Review* 29 (December): 1171–98.

O'Brien, Richard. 1992. *Global Financial Integration: The End of Geography.* New York: Council on Foreign Relations.

Oman, Charles. 1994. *Globalisation and Regionalisation: The Challenge for Developing Countries.* Paris: OECD Development Centre.

Panagariya, Arvind. 1993. "Should East Asia Go Regional? No, No, and Maybe." Mimeo. Washington: World Bank and University of Maryland.

———. 1994. "The Free Trade Area of the Americas: Good for Latin America?" Mimeo. University of Maryland.

Park, Yung Chul, and Jung Ho Yoo. 1989. "More Free Trade Areas: A Korean Perspective." In *Free Trade Areas and U.S. Trade Policy,* edited by Jeffrey J. Schott, 141–58. Washington: Institute for International Economics.

Peck, Merton J. 1989. "Industrial Organization and the Gains from Europe 1992." *Brookings Papers on Economic Activity* 2: 277–99.

Pelkmans, Jacques. 1992. Regionalism in World Trade: Vice or Virtue? Working Document 74. Brussels: Centre for European Policy Studies.

Perot, H. Ross, and Pat Choate. 1993. *Save Your Job, Save Our Country: Why NAFTA Must Be Stopped—Now!* Hyperion.

Perroni, Carlo, and John Whalley. 1994. *The New Regionalism: Liberalization or Insurance?* Working Paper 4626. Cambridge, Mass.: National Bureau of Economic Research.

Primo Braga, Carlos Alberto. 1992. "NAFTA and the Rest of the World." In *North American Free Trade,* edited by Nora Lustig, Barry P. Bosworth, and Robert Z. Lawrence, 210–49. Brookings.

Reinisch, August. 1993. "The European Economic Area." *Journal of Social, Political and Economic Studies* 18 (Fall): 279–309.

Sachs, Jeffery D., and Andrew Warner. 1995. "Economic Reform and the Process of Global Integration." *Brookings Papers on Economic Activity* 1: 1–118.

Sapir, André. 1992. "Regional Integration in Europe." *Economic Journal* (November): 1491–1506.

Sauvé, Pierre. 1994. "A First Look at Investment in the Final Act of the Uruguay Round." *Journal of World Trade* 28 (October): 5–16.

Saxonhouse, Gary R. 1993. "Pricing Strategies and Trading Blocks in East Asia." In *Regionalism and Rivalry: Japan and the United States in Pacific Asia,* edited by Jeffrey A. Frankel and Miles Kahler, 89–124. University of Chicago Press.

Schott, Jeffery. "More Free Trade Areas?" 1989. In *Free Trade Areas and U.S. Trade Policy,* edited by Jeffery J. Schott, 1–58. Washington: Institute for International Economics.

Scott, Norman. 1992. "The Commercial Policy of the European Economic Community." In *National Trade Policies: Handbook of Comparative Economic Policies,* vol. 2, edited by Dominick Salvatore, 31–56. Greenwood Press.

Segasti, F. R. 1990. "International Scientific and Technological Cooperation in a Fractured Global Order." United Nations Development Program, Roundtable on Global Development Challenges. New York (September).

Stoeckel, Andrew, David Pearce, and Gary Banks. 1990. *Western Trade Blocs: Game, Set or Match for Asia-Pacific and the World Economy?* Canberra: Centre for International Economics.

Tarr, David G. 1988. "The Steel Crisis in the U.S. and EC." In *Issues in U.S. - EC Trade Relations,* edited by Robert E. Baldwin, Carl B. Hamilton, and André Sapir, 173–98. University of Chicago Press.

Thurow, Lester C. 1992. *Head to Head: The Coming Economic Battle among Japan, Europe, and America.* William Morrow.

UN Centre on Transnational Corporations. 1991. *World Investment Report 1991: The Triad in Foreign Direct Investment.* New York: United Nations.

UN Conference on Trade and Development. 1994. *World Investment Report 1994: Transnational Corporations, Employment, and the Workplace.* New York.

UN Transnational Corporations and Management Division. 1992. *World Investment Report 1992: Transnational Corporations as Engines of Growth.* New York: United Nations.

Urata, Shujiro. "Japanese Foreign Direct Investment and Its Effect on Foreign Trade in Asia." 1993. In *Trade and Protectionism,* edited by Takatoshi Ito and Anne O. Krueger, 273–304. University of Chicago Press.

Vernon, Raymond. 1966. "International Investment and International Trade in the Product Cycle." *Quarterly Journal of Economics* 80 (May): 190–207.

———. 1994. "Multinationals and Governments: Key Actors in the NAFTA." In *Multinationals in North America,* edited by Lorraine Eden, 25–52. University of Calgary Press.

Viner, Jacob. 1950. *The Customs Union Issue.* New York: Carnegie Endowment for International Peace.

Wallace, William. 1994. *Regional Integration: The West European Experience.* Brookings.

Waverman, Leonard. 1991. "A Canadian Vision of North American Integration." In *Continental Accord: North American Economic Integration,* edited by Steven Globerman, 31–64. Vancouver: The Fraser Institute.

Wei, Shang-Jin, and Jeffrey Frankel. 1995. "Can Regional Blocs be Stepping Stones to Global Free Trade?" In *Review of International Economics and Finance.* Washington: Institute for International Economics. Forthcoming.

Wells, Louis T. 1992. *Mobile Exporters: The New Foreign Investors in East Asia.* Paper presented at the National Bureau of Economic Research Conference on Foreign Direct Investment.

Whalley, John. 1993. "Regional Trade Arrangements in North America: CUSTA and NAFTA." In *New Dimensions in Regional Integration,* edited by Jaime De Melo and Arvind Panagariya, 352–87. Cambridge University Press.

Wijkman, Per Magnus. 1992. "Trade Policies in Sweden." In *National Trade Policies: Handbook of Corporative Economic Policies,* vol. 2, edited by Dominick Salvatore, 285–310. Vol. 2. Greenwood Press.

Winters, Alan. 1992. "The European Community: A Case of Successful Regional Integration?" World Bank and CEPR Conference on New Dimensions in Regional Integration. Washington: World Bank.

Wonnacott, Paul. 1994. *Merchandise Trade in the APEC Region: Is There Scope for Liberalization on an MFN Basis?* Working Papers on Asia Pacific Economic Cooperation 94-4. Washington: Institute for International Economics.

Wonnacott, Paul, and Ronald Wonnacott. 1981. "Is Unilateral Tariff Reduction Preferable to a Customs Union? The Curious Case of the Missing Foreign Tariffs." *American Economic Review* 71 (September): 704–14.

Yamazawa, Ippei. 1993. *Economic Integration in the Asia Pacific and the Option for Japan.* Paper presented at MITI-RI Symposium.

Yi, Sang-Seung. 1994. "Stable Structures of Trading Blocs and Welfare." Mimeo. Dartmouth College.

Yokota, Kazuhiko, and Hideki Imaoka. 1993. "Structure of Trade Interdependence in Asia." In *Regional Integration and its Impact on Developing Countries,* edited by Koichi Ohno, 31–49. Tokyo: Institute of Developing Economies.

Young, Soogil. 1993. "Globalism and Regionalism: Complements or Competitors?" In *Pacific Dynamism and the International Economic System,* edited by C. Fred Bergsten and Marcus Noland, 111–31. Washington: Institute for International Economics.

Index